Trends in Organizational Behavior

Volume 4

Trends in Organizational Behavior

Volume 4

Edited by

Cary L. Cooper

Manchester School of Management, University of Manchester Institute of
Science and Technology, UK

and

Denise M. Rousseau

Carnegie-Mellon University, Pittsburgh, USA

JOHN WILEY & SONS

Chichester · New York · Weinheim · Brisbane · Singapore · Toronto

National   01243 779777
International   (+44) 1243 779777
e-mail (for orders and customer service enquiries): cs-books@wiley.co.uk
Visit our Home Page on http://www.wiley.co.uk
or http://www.wiley.com

Trends in Organizational Behavior, Volume 4

Published as a supplement to the
Journal of Organizational Behavior, Volume 18

Other Wiley Editorial Offices

John Wiley & Sons, Inc., 605 Third Avenue,
New York, NY 10158-0012, USA

VCH Verlagsgesellschaft mbH,
Pappelallee 3, 0-69469 Weinheim, Germany

Jacaranda Wiley Ltd, 33 Park Road, Milton,
Queensland 4064, Australia

John Wiley & Sons (Canada) Ltd, 22 Worcester Road,
Rexdale, Ontario M9W 1L1, Canada

John Wiley & Sons (Asia) Pte Ltd, 2 Clementi Loop #02-01,
Jin Xing Distripark, Singapore 129809

British Library Cataloguing in Publication data

A catalogue record for this book is available from the British Library

ISBN 0-471-97203-7

Typeset in 10/12pt Palatino by Mackreth Media Services, Hemel Hempstead, Herts
Printed and bound in Great Britain by Redwood Books, Trowbridge, Wiltshire
This book is printed on acid-free paper responsibly manufactured from sustainable forestation,
for which at least two trees are planted for each one used for paper production

Contents

About the Editors

CARY L. COOPER

Currently Professor of Organizational Psychology at the Manchester School of Management (UMIST) and Pro Vice Chancellor of the University of Manchester Institute of Science and Technology. Professor Cooper is the author of over 80 books (on stress, women at work, and industrial and organizational psychology), has written over 250 articles for academic journals, and is a frequent contributor to national newspapers, TV, and radio. Founding President of the British Academy of Management, he is currently Editor-in-Chief of the *Journal of Organizational Behavior*, and a Fellow of the British Psychological Society, Royal Society of Arts, The Royal Society of Medicine and the British Academy of Management. He is also Co-Editor, with Chris Argyris, of the twelve-volume *Encyclopedia of Management* (Blackwell).

DENISE M. ROUSSEAU

Denise Rousseau is a Professor of Organization Behavior at Carnegie-Mellon University, jointly in the Heinz School of Public Policy and Management and in the Graduate School of Industrial Administration. She has been a faculty member at Northwestern University, the University of Michigan, and the Naval Postgraduate School.

Her research addresses the impact of work group processes on performance and the changing psychological contract at work. Rousseau is an author of more than 60 articles which have appeared in prominent academic journals, such as the *Journal of Applied Psychology, Academy of Management Review,* and *Administrative Science Quarterly*. She is Associate Editor of the *Journal of Organizational Behavior*. Her books include: *Psychological Contracts in Organizations; Understanding Written and Unwritten Agreements* (Sage), the *Trends in Organizational Behavior* series

(Wiley) with Cary Cooper, *Developing an Interdisciplinary Science of Organizations* (Jossey-Bass) with Karlene Roberts and Charles Hulin, and *The Boundaryless Career* (Oxford) with Michael Arthur.

Professor Rousseau has consulted in diverse organizations and written numerous articles for managers and executives including "Teamwork: inside and out" (*Business Week/Advance*), "Managing diversity for high performance" (*Business Week/Advance*) and "Two ways to change (and keep) the psychological contract" (*Academy of Management Executive*). She has taught in executive programs at Northwestern (Kellogg), Cornell, Carnegie-Mellon and in industry programs for health care, journalism and manufacturing among others.

She is a Fellow in the American Psychological Association and Society for Industrial/Organizational Psychology, and serves on the Board of Governors for the Academy of Management.

Contributors

Ramona Bobocel	Department of Psychology, University of Waterloo, Waterloo, Ontario, CANADA, N2L 3C1
Arthur P. Brief	Lawrence Martin Chair of Business, A. B. Freeman School of Business, Tulane University, New Orleans, Louisiana 70118, USA.
Tony J. Chapman	Pro-Vice Chancellor, University of Leeds, Leeds, LS2 9JT, UK.
Daniel C. Feldman	University of South Carolina, South Carolina, USA.
Thomas A. Finholt	Department of Psychology, School of Business Administration, University of Michigan, Ann Arbor, Michigan 48109, USA.
Robert Folger	Department of Psychology, Tulane University, USA.
Charissa Freese	Department of Work and Organizational Psychology, WORC, Tilburg University, P.O. Box 90153, 5000 LE Tilburg, The Netherlands.
Erika L. Hayes	A. B. Freeman School of Business, Tulane University, New Orleans, Louisiana 70118, USA.
Carrie R. Leana	Katz Graduate School of Business, University of Pittsburg, 342 Mervis Hall, Pittsburgh, Pennsylvania 15260, USA.
Richard L. McCline	Department of Psychology, Tulane University, USA.
René Schalk	Department of Work and Organizational Psychology, WORC, Tilburg University, P.O. Box 90153, 5000 LE Tilburg, The Netherlands.
J. Silvester	University of Wales, Swansea, Wales, UK.
Phyllis Tharenou	Department of Business Management, Monash University, P.O. Box 197, Caulfield East, Victoria 3145, Australia.

William H. Turnley   University of South Carolina, South Carolina, USA.

Wang Zhong-Ming   School of Management, Hangzhou University, Hangzhou 320028, China.

Editorial Introduction

There is a plethora of books which provide comprehensive reviews of research on topics in industrial and organizational psychology and behavior, from the *Annual Review of Psychology* to the *International Review of Industrial and Organizational Psychology* to the *Handbook of I/O Psychology* to *Research in Organizational Behavior*. These volumes in different ways attempt to provide thorough and up-to-date accounts of research on particular topics or themes or methodological issues. Because of their need to survey an entire subject area (i.e. motivation, personnel, selection), they tend to concentrate on topics where there is substantial literature rather than focus on newly emerging fields, with the inevitable consequence that the massive literature reviewed submerges some interesting gem of research or material that might be of great importance to the wider public/private sector or practitioner constituency in organizational behavior and change. In other words, there is a gap in the literature in providing short, sharp accounts of research and practice which are published quickly and represent leading trends in organizational behavior (OB). This is the purpose of this volume and all those that will follow in this annual series. Although traditional topics of motivation, leadership, job design, personnel selection, etc., will be explored (probably in terms of a specific sub-topic issue), new and more innovative OB research toward issues reflecting the increasing interdependence in organizations (between persons, across groups and between work and homelife) will be primarily highlighted. Each short chapter will be a stand-alone topic, and there will be no attempt to integrate them into a theme. In a sense, the *Trends* volumes will be like a TV magazine program, with up-to-date issues explored in a short, hopefully incisive way and published swiftly—a kind of straight "off the press" OB research item.

In this fourth volume of the *Trends*, we have an array of eminent OB scholars from six countries around the world, Australia, Canada, China, Holland, the UK and the US. The chapters explore such issues as job loss, causal attributions and organizational behavior, determinants of participation in training and development, the electronic office, effective team management and cooperative decision making in Chinese organizations, affirmative action and fairness, new forms of organizational commitment and how organizational scholars can address the continuing issues to do with race in the workplace. These are broad ranging themes which cover some of the most important issues of our time, particularly about the electronic office, race at work, social policy in the workplace (e.g. affirmative action), coping with job loss and how the Chinese are using OB in their organizational life. These are meant to be stand-alone chapters, exploring potential research issues in OB for the future. We hope that you will find them stimulating and that they will contribute to your future research agenda.

CLC
DMR
July 1996

CHAPTER 1

Asking "Why?" in the Workplace: Causal Attributions and Organizational Behavior

J. Silvester
University of Wales, Swansea

and

A. J. Chapman
University of Leeds

We have all encountered an event at work which has made us stop and ask 'why?'. Unexpected praise from a manager, an unusual outburst by a colleague, organizational restructuring or surprising patterns of behavior from new team members, have all at some time or another left us searching for an explanation. Novel or potentially threatening events can be frequent occurrences in the work environment. They are also precisely the types of event most likely to trigger attributional activity, a process of "sense-making" whereby individuals attempt to identify the causes of such events in order to decide how best to respond (Baucom, 1987; Wong & Weiner, 1981). According to attribution theorists, people are motivated to make causal attributions because by doing so they render their environment more predictable and potentially more controllable (Heider, 1958). More specifically, workplace attributions have proved of interest to researchers because it is assumed that the way in which individuals explain events can have important consequences for how they choose to respond (e.g. Fincham & Jaspars, 1979).

There exists a substantial body of research concerned with workplace attributions and their role in moderating a diverse range of organizational behaviors—employee motivation and productivity (e.g. Corr & Gray, 1996; Seligman & Schulman, 1986), performance appraisal (e.g. Kipnis et al, 1981; Knowlton and Mitchell, 1980), selection decisions (Herriot, 1989; Silvester, in press; Struthers, Colwill and Perry, 1992), reactions to job loss (Prussia, Kinicki & Bracker, 1993; Winefield, Tiggemann & Winefield, 1992), and reactions to strategic responses by senior management (Dukerich & Nichols, 1991; Dutton & Jackson, 1987). However, this diversity can itself pose problems for the newcomer to the research field, and it is clear that a means of structuring the field is necessary in order for attributional research to continue to flourish. One attributional framework developed by Doise (1980) within social psychology particularly meets the needs of organizational researchers. Doise suggests that attributional activity takes place at four levels:

1. intra-personal attributions
2. interpersonal attributions
3. intergroup attributions
4. societal (organizational) attributions

LEVEL-1 OF ATTRIBUTIONAL ACTIVITY: INTRA-PERSONAL

"I didn't get the promotion because I don't know very much about that area."

Intra-personal attributions give rise to the explanations that an individual makes for his or her own behavior. The attributions reflect the individual's understanding of how his or her environment is organized, but can also be biased by personal and social–psychological factors; for example, through a desire to maintain self-esteem and a positive public image. In the workplace individual differences in attributional styles are important in behavior and motivation. Henry Ford's comment "failure is only the opportunity to begin again more intelligently" is a causal attribution neatly illustrating a distinction drawn by Seligman (1991) between an "optimistic" and a "pessimistic" attributional style: Ford was optimistic! Whereas optimists typically attribute positive outcomes to internal, stable and global causes, pessimists attribute them to external, unstable and specific causes. Moreover, because optimists (exemplified by Henry Ford) attribute negative outcomes and failure to external, unstable or specific causes, they are generally less vulnerable than pessimists (who attribute them to internal, stable and global causes) to feelings of helplessness. Consequently optimists continue to strive for success even when faced with persistent failure.

For insurance personnel, individual differences in attributional style have been found to predict sales performance: optimists have been found to sell significantly more insurance, and greater employee turnover has been observed in pessimists (Corr & Gray, 1996; Seligman & Schulman, 1986). There is evidence that, more generally, attributional style bears on the individual's reaction to unemployment and subsequent job-seeking behavior (e.g. Feather, 1983; Feather & Barber, 1983; Feather & Davenport, 1981; Miller & Hoppe, 1994). Winefield, Tiggemann and Winefield (1992) reported that unemployed individuals who attributed their job-loss to external causes (e.g. poor management of the company) possessed higher self-esteem and less hopelessness than those who attributed job-loss to internal causes such as lack of ability. Correspondingly, Prussia, Kinicki and Bracker (1993) found that individuals who one month beforehand attributed their job loss to internal and stable causes were less likely to have found a job eighteen months later.

LEVEL-2 OF ATTRIBUTIONAL ACTIVITY: INTERPERSONAL

"His failure to meet targets is down to a lack of motivation and insufficient effort."

In contrast to intra-personal attributions, where the focus is "self", interpersonal attributions are causal explanations for *another person's* behavior, and they are important moderators of interpersonal judgments and behavior. Beginning with selection procedures, interviewers' attributions for candidate behavior can influence recruitment decisions (Arvey & Campion, 1982; Herriot, 1989; Struthers, Colwill & Perry, 1992). When selling, the attributions made by a sales-person for a client's reaction have been shown to change the manner of engagement in the negotiation (Sujan, 1986). In the case of workplace attributions, most research has focused on supervisors' attributions for the causes of good and poor performance and decision-making about reward or punishment (e.g. Green & Mitchell, 1979; Heneman, Greenberger & Anonyuo, 1989). Underlying much of this research is an assumption that by identifying sources of bias in the attribution process, supervisor attributions can be rendered more "accurate", judgments more fair (Feldman, 1981; Gioia & Sims, 1986; Huber, Podsakoff & Todor, 1986) and consequently interactions more effective (Green & Mitchell, 1979). Consistent with that assumption, there is evidence that supervisors are more likely to use coercive powers and aggressive responses when poor performance is attributed to a "bad attitude" (internal, controllable causes), and that constructive explanation from supervisors is more likely when the cause is identified as an "inability" (Goodstadt & Kipnis, 1970). However, most evidence is gleaned from supervisors' attributions; virtually none is derived from subordinates' (Heneman, Greenberger and Anonyuo, 1989).

LEVEL-3 OF ATTRIBUTIONAL ACTIVITY: INTERGROUP

"Manufacturing are obsessed with detail. They don't realize that in sales we need a constant stream of new products in order to maintain our market share."

The quotation above illustrates a bias commonly found in "intergroup" attributions, also known as the "ultimate attributional error" (Pettigrew, 1979), namely a pervasive tendency for in-group members to maximize positive outcomes associated with their own group (the in-group) while minimizing those of the out-group. In the quotation a member of the sales team (in-group) attributes his or her team's difficulty in achieving targets to the manufacturing division's (out-group) focus on existing products rather than new-product development. Such "inter-group" attributions depend upon actual or perceived group membership. They are produced by members of a particular group for outcomes involving their own group and/or members of other groups (Hewstone, 1989). In-group members tend to attribute their own positive outcomes to internal, stable and potentially controllable causes; whereas outcomes which are positive to out-group members are likely to be attributed to external, unstable causes which are not under the control of the out-group member. Moreover, negative in-group outcomes are explained in terms of external, unstable and uncontrollable causes, and negative out-group outcomes to stable causes which are internal to the out-group and within their control (Hewstone, 1989; Pettigrew, 1979).

Intergroup attributions can increase conflict and reduce trust between groups, although such relationships may be moderated by the extent to which groups are dependent upon one another (Brown et al, 1986). Surprisingly little research, then, has investigated intergroup attributions between organizational departments or functions, or, indeed, across geographically dispersed groups. Given increasing globalization and the growing need for co-operation between geographically dispersed work-groups, an understanding of intergroup attributions and bias is important for creating and maintaining new forms of relationships. However, there have been inter-group attributions explorations with respect to gender, concluding that successful performance by women managers is more likely to be explained in terms of luck or effort than ability, and vice versa for men (Deaux & Emswiller, 1974). Race and intergroup attributions has been only sparsely researched, which is surprising given the level of unfair discrimination that occurs in the workplace (Silvester & Chapman, 1996).

LEVEL-4 OF ATTRIBUTIONAL ACTIVITY: ORGANIZATIONAL

"This company is committed to an open policy on information, so in general it is fairly easy to see how our work fits in with organizational strategy"

Our final level of attributional activity, described by Doise (1980) as "societal", refers to causal attributions which are shared by groups of people. For the work environment, we label these attributions "organizational": our interest lies in the extent to which attributions are shared by members of a specific organization or the sub-groups within that organization.

The investigation of organizational attributions has taken two directions. The first has explored how leaders and strategic planning groups identify and transmit the causes of successful and unsuccessful organizational performance to employees and to share-holders (Daft & Weick, 1984; Gooding & Kinicki, 1995; Smircich & Stubbart, 1985; Walsh, 1988). Attributions regarding the entry of new competitors into the market, increased staff turnover, and poor performance of the company are assumed to moderate decisions concerning presentation of strategy (Dukerich & Nichols, 1991; Dutton & Jackson, 1987). Senior managers' attributions for the causes of events can be distorted by common biases and may cause reduced levels of organizational performance (Clapham & Schwenk, 1991; Ford, 1985; Ford & Baucus, 1987).

The second direction of research has received less attention. It concerns relationships between socially shared attributions for important organizational events and the development of a cohesive organizational culture (e.g., Furnham, Sadka & Brewin, 1992; Moussavi & Evans, 1993). Organizational attributions are important because a shared understanding of the causes of specific organizational events, such as a change of strategy or a need to alter work practices, facilitates the development of collective schema, and that helps groups of people to respond in concert (Silvester et al, 1995). While some organizational attributions are adaptive, others are maladaptive. Martinko and Gardner (1982) argue that inadvertently organizations can sometimes induce a state of helplessness in employees through exposing them to persistent processes which are uncontrollable at an individual level, such as a long program of organizational "down-sizing".

FUTURE DIRECTIONS FOR ATTRIBUTION RESEARCH: ATTRIBUTIONS AS MODERATORS OF EFFECTIVE WORK RELATIONSHIPS

We have already suggested several areas worthy of further investigation, and now we select one area in particular, viz. attributions as moderators of effective work relationships. Traditional studies of supervisors' attributions for subordinate behavior have tended to explore issues of accuracy and fairness. Few have taken account of the relationship between supervisor and subordinate and even fewer the possible effects of interpersonal attributions (Heneman, Greenberger & Anonyuo, 1989; Martinko & Gardner, 1987; Tjosvold, 1985). Yet, there is increasing evidence that the way in which individuals explain their own and their partner's behavior is an important moderator of the quality of close personal relationships (Bradbury & Fincham, 1990; Fincham & Bradbury, 1987; Miller, 1995; Orvis, Kelley & Butler, 1976). Their explanations are central, not only to the development and maintenance of successful relationships but also to the exacerbation of conflict in distressed relationships (e.g. FIncham, Beach & Baucom, 1987). These observations have largely passed by organizational researchers, which is unfortunate given the possibility that similar attributional processes probably contribute to the development of relationships in the workplace.

Although effective work relationships are central to the successful functioning of an organization, and although a manager's ability to generate such relationships is a key determinant of managerial performance (Kotter, 1982; Liden & Graen, 1980), relatively little is known about how work relationships form (Gabarro, 1990). There are, admittedly, important differences between work relationships and close relationships; supervisors are expected to judge another's performance irrespective of whether he or she is "liked" (Wall & Adams, 1974). Unlike most close relationships, work relationships are formed for the purpose of task achievement, and they are judged using different criteria of success (Gabarro, 1990). But there are also important similarities. A "close relationship" is one in which there is strong, frequent and diverse interdependence in activities, thoughts and feelings between people, over an extended period (Harvey, 1987). Much the same often applies to "work relationships": interdependence, for example, is a salient aspect of supervisor–subordinate relationships, and it is an aspect which triggers the production of attributions (Hewstone, 1989). Hence findings from close-relationship research may illuminate our understanding of workplace behavior, recognizing that a person's role or job-description is itself an important determinant of behavior (Triandis, 1977).

The individual's attributions for his/her own behaviors and those of others contribute to the quality of personal relationships and act as predictors of subsequent levels of distress (Bradbury & Fincham, 1990; Fincham & Bradbury, 1987; Miller, 1995; Orvis, Kelley & Butler 1976). Typically in successful and in distressed relationships there are contrasting patterns of attributions for relationship events, and the clusters of attributes contribute to positive affect and/or levels of conflict. In successful relationships individuals generally attribute the partner's positive behavior to internal and stable causes like "personality", and their negative behavior to external, less controllable causes like circumstances or the behavior of another person (Fincham, Beach & Baucom, 1987). At the same time partners are more willing to accept responsibility for negative outcomes and take less personal credit for positive outcomes. Holtzworth-Munroe and Jacobsen (1985) describe this combination of attributions as "relationship-enhancing", in that it focuses attention on positive rather than negative outcomes and it increases levels of positive affect. By contrast, in highly distressed relationships, typified by high levels of conflict, individuals tend to attribute each other's negative behavior to more stable and controllable causes (e.g., "she makes sure that I never see the bills first") and positive behavior to external or unstable causes (e.g., "his brother had to remind him that it was my birthday"). More personal credit is taken for good events and responsibility is denied for negative ones, a pattern of attributions described as "distress-maintaining" because attention is focused on negative rather than positive behavior, resulting in negative affect and increased likelihood of conflict.

Similar patterns of attributions may likewise moderate levels of affect, cooperation and conflict within supervisor–subordinate relationships. Though Green and Mitchell (1979) suggested that empathy and liking might lead supervisors to make attributions for a subordinate which were more similar to those they made for themselves, few studies have investigated the transactional nature of attributions and the quality of workplace relationships. In a notable exception Fedor and Rowland (1989) observed that supervisor attributions for performance are influenced by psychological "distance" factors such as the supervisor's affective relationship with the employee. The longer and closer the working relationship, the more likely supervisors were to include

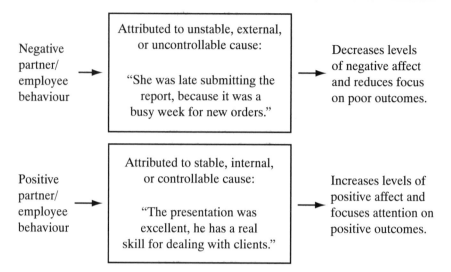

Figure 1.1   Relationship-enhancing attributional bias

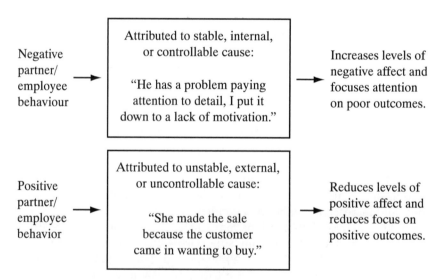

Figure 1.2   Distress-maintaining attributional bias

external influences in their evaluation of how much control subordinates could exert over their performance level. Unfortunately, Fedor and Rowland made no distinction between attributions for good and poor performance, an important omission given that in close relationships, external attributions increase for negative partner behavior in successful relationships, and decrease for positive behavior.

If attributions do reflect the quality of a relationship, it is to be expected that a manager who has a poor relationship with a subordinate is more likely to attribute poor subordinate performance to internal, stable and controllable causes (e.g., a lazy disposition) and good performance to external, unstable and less controllable causes (e.g., a positive economic climate). On the basis of relationship research, this manager would also be less likely to accept any personal responsibility (e.g., a failure to provide sufficient training) for the poor performance, and might take disproportionately more credit for any positive outcomes. Thus in a work relationship a polarization of attributions similar to that found in distressed close relationships may serve to maintain levels of distress, trust and conflict, and thereby contribute to unfair treatment, including blaming and scapegoating.

The converse pattern of attributions is characteristic of the most successful close relationships, with individuals attributing positive outcomes to partner and accepting more responsibility for negative outcomes. A "rose-tinted" attributional filter may be appropriate and functional in close relationships, but the workplace usually requires objectivity, to guard against favoritism and unfair treatment, and to ensure an appropriate perception of problems, development needs, and so forth. Effective work relationships are likely to depend upon the manager's ability to maintain a realistic assessment in the attributions made of others' behavior. Successful managers will accept responsibility for poor performance to the extent that they are responsible: they will give and take due credit.

INDIVIDUAL DIFFERENCES AND WORK RELATIONSHIPS

So far discussion has centered on the identification of nomothetic patterns of attributions which, it is argued, may typify successful and unsuccessful supervisor–subordinate relationships. However, equally important are individual differences in attributional style. For example, such differences can potentially predispose individuals to particular styles of management. In discussing adult and parent–child relationships Bugental et al. (1993) emphasize that individuals who objectively have high power within a relationship often present themselves as though at the mercy of a veridically lower-powered individual. In particular, abusive parents frequently see themselves as the "victim" of their child's uncontrollable behavior. Parents with self-perceptions of low control are more reactive to difficult child behavior and as a consequence adopt more coercive strategies (Bugental & Shennum, 1984). Similarly, adults who perceive caregiving outcomes as emanating from uncontrollable factors are more likely to regard children as potentially threatening and stress-inducing (Bugental, 1992). In contrast, adults who attribute caregiving failure to controllable factors behave little differently with responsive and unresponsive children (Bugental & Cortez, 1988). It is argued, then, that low-control attributions act in a sensitizing role and that high-control attributions act in a buffering role. There are connections with organizational research here: senior individuals in a work context who felt at a power disadvantage have been found more likely to exert high levels of coercion in an attempt to improve their perceptions of control (Raven & Kruglanski, 1970), and confident supervisors have been found more likely to seek to justify actions such as use of wage deductions, transfers or dismissals, and to use less coercive tactics (Goodstadt & Kipnis, 1970).

In some respects the supervisor–subordinate relationship is more reminiscent of a parent–child relationship than a close adult relationship. It is asymmetrical in terms of power (Gabarro, 1990), and supervisors, like parents, must understand their subordinates' actions in order to respond best. Managers are accountable, and poor subordinate performance may reflect badly upon the adequacy of a supervisor and be just as threatening to self-esteem as child misbehavior can be to a parent. In manager–subordinate relationships which involve a high degree of mutual dependency and where the manager's performance is more directly tied to their ability to motivate and encourage a subordinate the relationship becomes crucial (Ilgen, Mitchell & Fredrickson, 1981). However, differences in the level of control that individual managers perceive themselves able to exert within their role may sensitize them, in the case of low perceived control, or buffer them, in the case of high perceived control, to difficult or poor subordinate performance. Managers who perceive themselves to have little control may be more reactive to poor subordinate performance, more likely to engage in coercive behavior and more vulnerable to engaging in "distress-maintaining" patterns of attributions. Thus, focus is shifted away from a relatively simple consideration of the accuracy of managers' attributions to the more complex transactional relationship between behavior, quality of relationship, individual differences in perceived control and defensive patterns of attributions.

CONCLUSIONS

Clearly attribution theory has already provided a valuable insight into how and when people engage in organizational sense-making as well as the behavioral consequences of asking "why?" at work. Yet it is also clear that there is still much to be learnt, particularly in the area of attributions and work relationships. Furthermore, the changing patterns of work which are a feature of the 1990s are likely to have profound effects upon the way in which people interact with one another. Here, too, an attributional focus may provide dividends; for example, new ways of working are likely to have profound effects upon the way people form relationships and cooperate in organizations. The very rapid advances that have been made recently in the areas of computer and telecommunication technology have provided organizations with the means to restructure, and to become increasingly global and dispersed. Just one of the many consequences for some managers has been a need to engage in "tele-management"—the supervision of employees in different geographical locations (Huws, Korte & Robinson, 1990). These changes raise important issues with respect to the nature of management relationships in the future and pose new questions for researchers interested in how work relationships develop. Attribution research presents one important means by which these new relationships, facilitated through communication media, such as video-conferencing and email, can be explored. Researchers interested in the development of work relationships would do well to look to the considerable body of research concerned with attributions and close relationships. The task will be to draw parallels and identify dissimilarities between these relationships and the ones that develop in the workplace.

REFERENCES

Arvey, R. D. & Campion, J. E. (1982) The employment interview: A summary and review of recent research. *Personnel Psychology*, **35**, 281–323.

Baucom, D. H. (1987) Attributions in distressed relationships: How can we explain them? In D. Perlman and S. Duck (Eds), *Intimate Relationships: Development, Dynamics and Deterioration*. London: Sage.

Bradbury, T. N. & Fincham, F. D. (1990) Attributions in marriage: A review and critique. *Psychological Bulletin*, **107**, 3–33.

Brown, R. J., Condor, S. Matthews, A., Wade, G. & Williams, J. (1986) Explaining intergroup differentiation in an industrial organization. *Journal of Occupational Psychology*, **59**, 273–286.

Bugental, D. B. (1992) Affective and cognitive processes within threat-oriented family systems. In I. E. Sigel, A. V. McGillicuddy-DeLisi and J. J. Goodnow (Eds), *Parental Belief Systems: The Psychological Consequences for Children* (2nd edn). Hillsdale NJ: Erlbaum.

Bugental, D. B., Blue, J., Cortez, V., Fleck, K., Kopeikin, H., Lewis, J. C. & Lyon, J. (1993) Social cognitions as organizers of autonomic and affective responses to social challenge. *Journal of Personality and Social Psychology*, **64**, 94–103.

Bugental, D. B. & Cortez, V. L. (1988) Physiological reactivity to responsive and unresponsive children as moderated by perceived control. *Child Development,* **59,** 686–693.

Bugental, D. B. & Shennum, W. A. (1984) "Difficult" children as elicitors and targets of adult communication patterns: An attributional–behavioral transactional analysis. *Monographs for the Society for Research into Child Development,* **49** (1), Serial no. 205.

Clapham, S. E. & Schwenk, C. R. (1991) Self-serving attributions, managerial cognition and company performance. *Strategic Management Journal,* **12,** 212–219.

Corr, P. J. & Gray, J. A. (1996) Attributional style as a personality factor in insurance sales performance in the UK. *Journal of Occupational and Organizational Psychology,* **69,** 83–87.

Daft, R. L. & Weick, K. E. (1984) Toward a model of organizations as interpretation systems. *Academy of Management Review,* **9,** 284–295.

Deaux, K. & Emswiller, T. (1974) Explanations of successful performance on sex-limited tasks: What is skill for the male is luck for the female. *Journal of Personality and Social Psychology,* **29,** 80–85.

Doise, W. (1980) Levels of explanation. *European Journal of Social Psychology,* **10,** 213–231.

Dukerich, J. M. & Nichols, M. L. (1991) Causal information search in managerial decision making. *Organizational Behavior and Human Decision Processes,* **50,** 106–122.

Dutton, J. E. & Jackson, S. E. (1987) Categorizing strategic issues: Links to organizational action. *Academy of Management Review,* **12,** 76–90.

Feather, N. T. (1983) Some correlates of attributional style: Depressive symptoms, self-esteem and protestant ethic values. *Personality and Social Psychology Bulletin,* **9,** 125–135.

Feather, N. T. & Barber, J. G. (1983) Depressive reactions and unemployment. *Journal of Abnormal Psychology,* **92,** 185–195.

Feather, N. T. & Davenport, P. R. (1981) Unemployment and depressive affect: A motivational and attributional analysis. *Journal of Personality and Social Psychology,* **41,** 422–436.

Fedor, D. B. & Rowland, K. M. (1989) Investigating supervisor attributions of subordinate performance. *Journal of Management,* **15,** 405–416.

Feldman, J. M. (1981) Beyond attribution theory: Cognitive processes in performance appraisal. *Journal of Applied Psychology,* **66,** 127–148.

Fincham, F. D., Beach, S. & Baucom, D. (1987) Attribution processes in distressed and non-distressed couples 2: Self-partner attribution differences. *Journal of Personality and Social Psychology,* **52,** 739–748.

Fincham, F. D. & Bradbury, T. N. (1987) The impact of attributions in marriage: A longitudinal analysis. *Journal of Personality and Social Psychology,* **53,** 510–517.

Fincham, F. D. & Jaspars, J. (1979) Attribution of responsibility to the self and other in children and adults. *Journal of Personality and Social Psychology,* **37,** 1589–1602.

Ford, J. D. (1985) The effects of causal attributions on decision makers' responses to performance downturns. *Academy of Management Review,* **10,** 770–786.

Ford, J. D. & Baucus, D. A. (1987) Organizational adaptation to performance downturns: An interpretation-based perspective. *Academy of Management Review,* **12,** 366–380.

Furnham, A., Sadka, V. & Brewin, C. R. (1992) The development of an Occupational Attributional Style Questionnaire. *Journal of Organizational*

Behavior, **13**, 27–39.

Gabarro, J. J. (1990) The development of working relationships. In J. Galegher, R. E. Kraut and C. Egido (eds), *Intellectual Teamwork*. New Jersey: Erlbaum. pp 79–110.

Gioia, D. A. & Sims, H. P. (1986) Cognition–behavior connections: Attribution and verbal behavior in leader–subordinate interactions. *Organizational Behavior and Human Decision Processes*, **37**, 197–229.

Gooding, R. Z. & Kinicki, A. J. (1995) Interpreting event causes: The complementary role of categorization and attribution processes. *Journal of Management Studies*, **32**, 1–22.

Goodstadt, B. & Kipnis, D. (1970) Situational influence on the use of power. *Journal of Applied Psychology*, **54**, 201–207.

Green, S. G. & Mitchell, T. R. (1979) Attributional processes of leader–member interactions. *Organizational Behavior and Human Performance*, **23**, 429–458.

Harvey, J. H. (1987) Attributions in close relationships: Research and theoretical developments. *Journal of Social and Clinical Psychology*, **5**, 420–434.

Heider, F. (1958) *The Psychology of Interpersonal Relations*. New York: Wiley.

Heneman, R. L., Greenberger, D. B. & Anonyuo, C. (1989) Attributions and exchanges: The effects of interpersonal factors on the diagnosis of employee performance. *Academy of Management Journal*, **32**, 466–476.

Herriot, P. (1989) Attribution theory and interview decisions. In R. W. Eder and G. R. Ferris (eds), *The Employment Interview: Theory, Research and Practice*. London: Sage.

Hewstone, M. (1989) *Causal Attribution: From Cognitive Processes to Collective Beliefs*. Oxford: Blackwell.

Holtzworth-Munroe, A. & Jacobsen, N. S. (1985) Causal attributions for married couples: When do they search for causes? What do they conclude when they do? *Journal of Personality and Social Psychology*, **48**, 1398–1412.

Huber, V. L., Podsakoff, P. M. & Todor, W. D. (1986) An investigation of biasing in the attributions of subordinates and their supervisors. *Journal of Business Research*, **14**, 83–98.

Huws, U., Korte, W. & Robinson, S. (1990) *Telework: Towards the Elusive Office*. Chichester: Wiley.

Ilgen, D. R., Mitchell, T. R. & Fredrickson, J. W. (1981) Poor performers: Supervisors' and subordinates' responses. *Organizational Behavior and Human Performance*, **27**, 386–410.

Kipnis, D. S., Schmidt, K., Price, K. & Stitt, C. (1981) Why do I like thee: Is it your performance or my orders? *Journal of Applied Psychology*, **66**, 324–328.

Knowlton, W. A. & Mitchell, T. R. (1980) Effects of causal attribution on a supervisor's evaluation of subordinate performance. *Journal of Applied Psychology*, **65**, 459–466.

Kotter, J. P. (1982) *The General Managers*. New York: Macmillan.

Liden, R. C. & Graen, C. (1980) Generalizability of the vertical dyad linkage model of leadership. *Academy of Management Journal*, **23**, 451–465.

Martinko, M. J. & Gardner, W. L. (1982) Learned helplessness: An alternative explanation for performance deficits. *Academy of Management Review*, **7**, 413–417.

Martinko, M. J. & Gardner, W. L. (1987) The leader/member attribution process. *Academy of Management Review*, **12**, 235–249.

Miller, M. V. & Hoppe, S. K. (1994) Attributions for job termination and psychological distress. *Human Relations*, **47**, 307–327.

Miller, S. A. (1995) Parents' attributions for their children's behavior. *Child Development*, **66**, 1557–1584.

Moussavi, F. & Evans, D. A. (1993) Emergence of organizational attributions. The role of shared cognitive schema. *Journal of Management*, **19**, 79–95.

Orvis, B. R., Kelley, H. H. & Butler, D. (1976) Attributional conflict in young couples. In J. H., Harvey, W. Ickes, and R. Kidd, (eds), *New Directions in Attribution Research*, Vol. 1. Hillsdale NJ: Erlbaum.

Prussia, G. E., Kinicki, A. J. & Bracker, J. S. (1993) Psychological and behavioral consequences of job loss: A covariance structure analysis using Weiner's (1985) attribution model. *Journal of Applied Psychology*, **78**, 382–394.

Raven, B. H. & Kruglanski, A. W. (1970) Conflict and power. In P. Swingle (ed), *The Structure of Conflict*. New York: Academic Press.

Seligman, M. E. P. (1991) *Learned Optimism*. New York: Knopf.

Seligman, M. E. P. & Schulman, P. (1986) Explanatory style as a predictor of productivity and quitting among life insurance sales agents. *Journal of Personality and Social Psychology*, **50**, 832–838.

Silvester, J. (in press) Spoken attributions and candidate success in graduate recruitment interviews. *Journal of Occupational and Organizational Psychology*.

Silvester, J. & Chapman, A. J. (1996) Unfair discrimination in the selection interview: An attributed account. *International Journal of Selection and Assessment*, **4**, 63–70.

Silvester, J., Patterson, F., Anderson, N. & Ferguson, E. (1995) Unlocking the quality culture: A socio-cognitive model of organizational culture and culture change. *Paper presented at the Annual Occupational Psychology Conference of the British Psychological Society, Warwick, January.*

Smircich, L. and Stubbart, C. (1985) Strategic management in an enacted world. *Academy of Management Review*, **10**, 724–736.

Struthers, C. W., Colwill, N. L. and Perry, R. P. (1992) An attributional analysis of decision making in a personnel selection interview. *Journal of Applied Social Psychology*, **22**, 801–818.

Sujan, H. (1986) Smarter versus harder: An exploratory attributional analysis of sales people's motivation. *Journal of Marketing Research*, **23**, 41–49.

Tjosvold, D. (1985) The effects of attribution and social context on superiors' influence and interaction with low performing subordinates. *Personnel Psychology*, **38**, 361–376.

Triandis, H. C. (1977) *Interpersonal Behavior*. Monterey, CA: Brooks/Cole.

Wall, J. A. and Adams, J. S. (1974) Some variables affecting a constituent's evaluations of and behavior toward a boundary-role occupant. *Organizational Behavior and Human Performance*, **2**, 290–308.

Walsh, J. P. (1988) Selectivity and selective perception: An investigation of managers' belief structures and information processing. *Academy of Management Journal*, **31**, 873–896.

Winefield, A. H., Tiggemann, M., and Winefield, H. R. (1992) Unemployment distress, reasons for job loss and causal attributions for unemployment in young people. *Journal of Occupational and Organizational Psychology*, **65**, 213–218.

Wong, P. T. P. and Weiner, B. (1981) When people ask "why" questions and the heuristics of attribution search. *Journal of Personality and Social Psychology*, **40**, 649–663.

CHAPTER 2

Determinants of Participation in Training and Development

Phyllis Tharenou
Monash University, Australia

Training is regarded as critical to employee skill acquisition, and has been shown to improve productivity at organizational (Bartel, 1994) and individual (Guzzo, Jette & Katzell, 1985) levels. Similar to the approach used for decades in Japan (e.g., Robinson & Stern, 1995), governments in the US (e.g., US Department of Labor, 1989), Australia (e.g. Dawkins, 1989), and the UK (Heseltine in Littlefield, 1995) have recently implemented policies to increase training, in order to be competitive in the global economy. Participation in training has indeed increased (Anon, 1995; Organization for Economic Cooperation and Development [OECD], 1993). However, some employees are reluctant to attend training (e.g. Australian Bureau of Statistics [ABS], 1993) and some employers to provide it, as shown in Europe, the US and Australia (Holden, 1993; OECD, 1993). What causes attendance at training and development once employees qualify for their jobs is not understood (see review by Scott & Meyer, 1991).

Participation in training may be influenced by group membership. Those with disabilities or born in non-English-speaking countries gain less training and development than others, for example, in Australia (ABS, 1993). Although women in the US, UK, and Australia have gained as frequent or more training than men (ABS, 1993; Gibbins, 1994; Veum, 1996), they gain less training time and different types of training (ABS, 1993; Altonji & Spletzer, 1991; Booth, 1991). The differential training of some employee groups is a significant issue in terms of access and equity in society. Training increases employment duration and continuity (e.g., Gritz, 1993) and managerial advancement, but leads to less managerial advancement for women than men (for a review, see Tharenou, 1997a).

Trends in Organizational Behavior, Volume 4. Edited by C. L. Cooper and D. M. Rousseau.
© 1997 John Wiley & Sons Ltd.

For training to be increased in the ways intended by government for productivity and equity, determinants of participation in training and development therefore need to be understood.

The studies conducted of participation in training are from two distinct streams, neither of which provide sufficient empirical explanation. The labor market studies, based on human capital theory, assess person attributes (e.g., age, education, work tenure) and job and industry types for their link to training, measured as any type of training and development activity by different, noncomparable measures (e.g., Booth, 1991, 1993; Green, 1993). The second research stream, from a psychological basis, explains participation only in development, as a separate category. Development activities are for personal and professional growth and the long term (Noe & Wilk, 1993) including updating and continuous learning (Noe & Ford, 1992), whereas training consists of systematic activities for improving performance in the current job and short term. The psychological explanations assess the influence of employee attitudes towards training and the perceived work environment on development. When the psychological studies have included a limited number of human capital or job attributes, explanation has increased substantially (Kozlowski & Hults, 1987; Noe, 1996; Noe & Wilk, 1993). Research thus needs to be innovative by combining labor market approaches from a human capital view and psychological approaches from work environment and employee attitude views to explain participation, overall and comparatively, in training and in development. The labor market and psychological factors fall into individual, job and organizational level categories, consistent with the categories in training needs analysis.

ANTECEDENTS OF PARTICIPATION IN TRAINING AND DEVELOPMENT

Personal Level Factors

Human capital. According to human capital theory (Becker, 1975), employees invest in training to learn or improve skills to increase pay, and employers invest in training employees to improve productivity, and thus more in firm-specific than general training. The impact of human capital should be greater on training (more firm-specific) than development (more general). Indeed, participation in training and development is greater for those:

- more educated, including when controlling for ability (e.g., Altonji & Spletzer, 1991; Baker & Wooden, 1992; Green, 1993; Veum, 1996), who are thought to have more aptitude and willingness to be trained than those less educated;

• younger (e.g., Baker & Wooden, 1992; Booth, 1991) rising to middle-aged and then declining (Baker & Wooden, 1992), for whom investment in training can be recouped than for those older.

Training is less for:

• women with young children and spouses (Booth, 1991; Green, 1991, 1993), who are thought less able to be more committed to paid labor than others because of family-caring responsibilities.

Human capital factors may be relatively unimportant when other factors are taken into account. In tests controlling occupation skill levels (Altonji & Spletzer, 1991; Tharenou, 1977b), human capital factors reduced in impact on participation in training and development. Under-represented groups also need to be examined. For example, job tenure advantaged men's training more than women's (Green, 1993; Tharenou Latimer & Conroy, 1994), but education, at least at low hierarchical levels, appeared to advantage women (Booth, 1991; Green, 1993).

Employee attitudes. Employees with positive attitudes to training should participate more, with development examined but not training. Development is found greater for employees with high motivation to learn and to transfer training to the job, high development needs, and high career exploration and insight, although effects are inconsistent (Maurer & Tarulli, 1994; Noe & Wilk, 1993; Tharenou, 1997) and some nonsignificant for predicting future development (Noe, 1996). Motivation to learn may have most consistent effects. Self-efficacy had positive but weak effects on participation in development (Maurer & Tarulli, 1994; Noe & Wilk, 1993), suggesting employees who feel confident to undertake the challenges of training participate more than others. Employees high in masculine gender role, and thus instrumental in orientation, gained more training and development a year later (Tharenou, 1997b). Some attitudes that appear relevant, such as employee evaluation of past training and development and employee training and development needs, have been little researched. Longitudinal studies and reciprocal tests are rarely conducted, even though past participation in training and development may influence attitudes towards training.

The nature of the relationships between training attitudes and participation is not clear. Training attitudes have been shown to have direct effects on participation in development, and not to be mediators as proposed (in which training policies would influence training attitudes which in turn influence participation) (Noe & Wilk, 1993). By contrast, supporting moderator effects, when employee values specifically matched the nature of training policies and supervisor support, participation in development was higher (Maurer & Tarulli, 1994).

Theorists argue for the central importance of training attendance motivation (that is, employee expectancies of costs and benefits from participation), for development as updating or continuous learning in which employees voluntarily develop themselves (Dublin, 1990; Farr & Middlebrooks, 1990; Noe & Ford, 1992). If employees believe the benefits of training or development outweigh its costs, they should seek and accept participation. Australians report that the major reason they did not attend training in work time was that it made little difference to work prospects (ABS, 1993). Employees who perceived training as providing benefits of personal development and career goals and outcomes participated more in development than others (Maurer & Tarulli, 1994; Noe & Wilk, 1993), as did those further from their career goal (Noe, 1996), presumably because development would help them reach it. The measures have directly asked employees about the benefits of training, rather than, from an expectancy theory framework, the combined influence of employee expectancies that participating in training and development:

- will result in successful training performance (e.g., skills);
- that is instrumental for gaining outcomes (e.g., advancement);
- that they value rather than not value.

Training attendance motivation should directly predict actual participation in training and development. It may do so directly in addition to the work environment (Dublin, 1990), or the work environment may influence participation through effects on training attendance motivation (Farr & Middlebrooks, 1990). Training attendance motivation should influence development more than training because it is more dependent on individual choice.

Job Level Factors

Jobs are structured into types that vary in skill level, according to the range and complexity of their duties, in a way that should systematically and directly influence the training needed to perform the job, and thus the opportunity for training, and the training received (Tharenou, 1997b). Occupations with higher skill levels are also proposed to provide more returns to the organization from training from a human capital view (Green, 1993), and so should be afforded more training. Skill requirements are the basis for standardized occupational classifications, providing occupation types which decrease in the range and complexity of duties in the order of managers, professionals, paraprofessionals, tradespersons, clerks, sales and personal service workers, and laborers. Occupational types reflect the primary versus secondary labor market, the former providing career paths and job security. Managerial level is also likely to be related to participation in training and development because, as managerial jobs increase in level, they have higher level skill requirements, thus directly influencing need and therefore opportunity to participate.

In support, training and development decreased in occupations from higher to lower skill levels, for example, from managerial and professional to clerical and technical (e.g., Baker & Wooden, 1992; Green, 1991, 1993). Being in a managerial occupation or not was related to participation in development, as much as or more than organizational and personal factors (Noe, 1996; Noe & Wilk, 1993) and to training hours but not frequency (Veum, 1996). Managerial/nonmanagerial status (Noe, 1996) and managerial level (Tharenou, 1997b) have predicted future development, taking into account individual and organizational factors. The studies of development have generally considered job factors in an *ad hoc* unsystematic way and have not conducted tests of several, theoretically relevant job factors. Consistent with primary versus secondary jobs, a study of 20 manufacturing plants found that skills training for advanced technologies and contemporary production techniques was highest in organizations with institutionalized internal labor markets than others, in which training did not occur or was superficial (Hodson, Hooks, & Rieble, 1994).

Behavioral job characteristics such as variety and autonomy should increase the mental skill requirements of jobs and the number and level of skills involved (Campion & Berger, 1990), requiring employees to be trained and developed. Job challenge as measured by behavioral job characteristics was a key factor predicting participation in development of engineers a year later (Kozlowski & Farr, 1988). The theory is that jobs with high challenge require use of a repertoire of skills and development of new skills. A job characteristics approach assessing job complexity should therefore also be examined as explanatory of participation in training and development, also reflecting skill requirements. The importance of variety, autonomy and "whole" tasks for gaining training and development reflects the multiskilling required for self-managing teams (Anon, 1995; Cusimano, 1995), and the broadbanding and award restructuring from amalgamation of job classifications, for example, in Australia (Dawkins, 1989).

Job level factors should most explain why underrepresented groups gain fewer hours of training and development (i.e., duration) than others, and be more explanatory than personal and organizational factors. Women may gain as frequent, or more frequent, training and development than men because they are in job types that require more short training courses than other job types. However, women are likely to gain fewer hours per year of training and development than men because they are likely to be:

- clerks and sales and personal service workers rather than managers and administrators and tradespersons, as men are (ABS, 1992), the former occupations being lower in skill level;
- at lower managerial levels (Tharenou, 1997a); and
- in jobs having shorter duration of training time (Barron, Black, & Loewenstein, 1992).

Training and development may also be less for those with disabilities and from non-English-speaking backgrounds than others because of the types of jobs held. Occupation type and group membership (e.g., gender, ethnicity) are confounded, resulting in the impact on training and development of group membership being difficult to disentangle from job type. Hence, to compare predictors of participation in training and development by group membership, the subgroups (e.g., English versus non-English speaking background) need to be comparable on job level factors through sampling (stratified, matching), or statistical interactions used to assess if the impact of the job factor is dependent on the subgroup. The policy implications if job factor effects for subgroups are supported are that training and development duration will increase only with changed occupation choice, job placement, or job redesign.

Organizational Level Factors

The two types of organizational factors examined have been organization characteristics—size, public/private sector, and industry—and the perceived work environment. Organization size (Baker & Wooden, 1992; Frazis, Herz, & Horrigan, 1995), allowing economies of scale, and the public rather than private sector (Baker & Wooden, 1992; Tharenou, 1997b), enabling fewer market fluctuations, are positively related to participation in training and development.

The impact of the perceived work environment for supporting training and development—supervisor behaviors, peer interactions, work assignments, training policies, and climate—has been examined chiefly on participation in development, requiring research on training. Direct effects are either proposed, with employees thought to participate in development if they perceive a supportive work environment for training (Dublin, 1990; Kozlowski & Farr, 1988), or mediated effects through training attitudes (Farr & Middlebrooks, 1990; Noe & Wilk, 1993) which in the one test did not gain support (Noe & Wilk, 1993). When training policies and climate have been related to participation in development, the links are direct, but they are also inconsistent and usually weaker than those of human capital, training attitudes, and job level factors (e.g., Kozlowski & Hults, 1987; Noe & Wilk, 1993; Tharenou, 1997b). Supervisor and peer support for development are also weakly related to participation in development (e.g., Kozlowski & Hults, 1987; Maurer & Tarulli, 1994; Noe & Wilk, 1993), although manager support and feedback (Noe, 1996) and supervisor and peer career encouragement (Tharenou, 1997b) predicted future development. It may be that career feedback and encouragement influences seeking, or accepting opportunities for training and development, and that organizations with a "career culture" increase training and development.

The generally weak effects of the work environment may occur because it does not have such direct, proximal effects on opportunities for training and development as do human capital and job factors. Policies may not translate into practice, as shown by developmental performance appraisal programs not increasing appraisee training and development (e.g., Tharenou, 1995). The work environment factors that should be most related to participation in development would be those that make it possible to attend and that reduce barriers and situational constraints, with some evidence supportive (Maurer & Tarulli, 1994; Noe & Wilk, 1993). This is consistent with employee reasons for nonparticipation in terms of lack of time and no courses being available (ABS, 1993).

Factors at the overall organizational level are rarely examined. Organizations that emphasize training and development in their business strategy should increase employee participation (e.g., Holden, 1993; OECD, 1993). Training should be integrated with business strategy, and to follow the strategic plan. Strategic business issues have been linked to executives' participation in development (Seibert, Hall & Kram, 1995), but not to employees' participation in training and development, although the link was found more in high technology organizations and the public sector than other organization types (Rainbird, 1994). Organization change that emphasizes increasing organizational performance, service/customer orientation, and flexibility, when combined with organization downsizing and decentralizing, would result in employee training and development to cope with multiskilled, responsive, customer-oriented jobs (e.g., Pizza Hut in the UK, Thatcher, 1995). US organizations that use more high-performance work place practices (e.g., self-managing teams, quality management, compensation for knowledge, employee incentive schemes, information systems and decision participation), requiring a commitment to training for their successful adoption, reported greater employee participation in training than others (Frazis, Herz & Horrigan, 1995). For instance, increased technical, interpersonal and team skills training was needed for Coca-Cola's continuous improvement teams (Phillips, 1996). Moreover, a cost reduction business strategy or poor organizational profitability may reduce opportunities for training and development.

Future Research

The antecedents of training and of development need to be examined separately. They are often conducted for different groups and purposes (Noe et al, 1996), and are likely to have different antecedents. For instance, human capital and job level factors should predict training more than development and training attendance motivation should predict development more than training. The organizational approaches used, and individual attitudes needed, for development as continuous learning should differ from traditional human resource approaches (Noe & Ford, 1992), and thus presumably from antecedents for training for the current job. Training measures need to be differentiated from development and focus on job-related, skills-based, short-term or firm-specific activities, such as job-specific training courses and seminars, induction, systematic coaching, and training for skills for the current job (e.g., word processing, technical skills, communication, mandatory skills), for new methods and equipment, for quality improvement, and for the specific job type (e.g., first-line supervisor, clerk, customer service and sales occupations, manager). Multi-item scales should be used for training, as in recent studies of development (e.g., Maurer & Tarulli, 1994; Noe, 1996; Tharenou, 1997b), rather than the chiefly single-item measures used (e.g., Green, 1991, 1993). However, the development scales need to measure actual participation, rather than seeking it (e.g., Noe, 1996), and comprehensively, rather than using a limited number of activities (Tharenou, 1997b). The activities should be long-term, personally and professionally oriented activities, including courses, workshops, and seminars, industry meetings and conferences, committees, work assignments (special projects, task force membership), job assignments (job rotation, transfers, secondments, acting in higher positions), mentoring, career planning, and continuing education and study assisted schemes.

Future research needs to assess the relative contribution of personal (human capital, training attitudes, family), job, and organizational factors to future participation in training and in development, and extend the variables considered because very little variance has been explained in training (e.g., Green, 1993) or development (e.g., Kozlowski & Hults, 1987; Noe, 1996; Tharenou, 1997b). Personal and job factors, because of their proximal and direct influences, should more strongly predict participation in training and development than should organizational level factors, although human capital may decrease in influence with job factors controlled. There needs to be a systematic examination of several job level factors (occupation type, managerial level, job characteristics), because they are directly linked to training opportunity. For this reason, they are likely to predict participation in training more than do individual factors, such as training attitudes. Relevant training attitudes less researched hitherto such as training attendance motivation and evaluation of past training and development activities need to be assessed. The work environment (training policies, situational barriers, interpersonal support) may have little effect once personal and job level effects are taken into account. The impact of training barriers and organizational factors rarely examined—those of training strategy, high performance practices, and organizational profitability—need to be assessed. Work environment factors have been measured either at overall organization levels in an objective fashion (e.g., size) or at more immediate levels by employee self-report. The immediate environment should also be measured other than by self-report (e.g., supervisor perceptions) and the overall organizational environment by executives' assessments (e.g., of training strategy) and company information (e.g., company annual reports for profitability and human resources practices). Longitudinal data are required to examine if future participation can be predicted, with the few longitudinal psychological studies showing weak inconsistent effects (Kozlowski & Farr, 1988; Noe, 1996; Tharenou, 1997b).

The relative importance of organizational, job and personal level factors should be examined for underrepresented groups, including by gender, ethnic background, and disability, the latter two apparently unresearched. Job level factors should most explain the training and development of women and those from ethnic backgrounds, rather than personal and organizational factors, although one study did not support gender differences (Tharenou, 1997b). Group factors also need to be examined in combination. For instance, migrant or black women or women with disabilities may gain less participation in training and development than others.

The nature of the link (direct, moderator, mediator, reverse) between attitudes relevant to training attendance (e.g., motivation to learn, training and development needs, career strategies, evaluation of past training and development, training attendance motivation) and participation in training and development needs to be determined. Future research needs to examine moderator effects of training attitudes on participation in training and development, because they provide a theoretically plausible explanation for the lack of support for mediated effects, and the little support for direct effects of the work environment. For example, for employees more rather than less motivated to learn, organizational policies to facilitate training attendance or practices to remove constraints should increase participation in training and in development. The impact of training attitudes on participation in training and development needs to be assessed using longitudinal repeated data collections enabling testing of bidirectional links.

"Causal" models of participation in training or in development need to be developed because multivariate explanations and direct and moderator effects are suggested. Models should be developed from an interactive sequence of paths linking the work environment, training attitudes, job factors, human capital, and family factors, using selected variables, and tested for the total sample and by intragroup comparisons (e.g., gender), predicting that explanatory processes will differ. As shown in Figure 2.1, the work environment (e.g., organization situation constraints, training attendance policy) should either directly influence or interact with training attitudes (motivation to learn). Family variables and age should influence work tenure (e.g., differently for women and men), and education should increase job factors (occupation skill level). In turn, the work environment, job factors, training attitudes, and human capital should directly influence participation in training and development.

Conclusion and Practical Implications

Participation in training and development appears highest when employees are at high managerial levels or in highly skilled occupations, are high in education level and younger rather than older, have high motivation to learn and perceive career benefits from training, and are in organizations that facilitate attendance at training and development and reduce barriers, encourage career development, and are larger rather than smaller. Job and personal level factors appear to have most impact. However, much research needs to be done. Organizations should target training programs at relevant, specific job, personal and organizational factors to increase employee attendance, especially for groups under-represented at high organizational levels, and especially focusing on job

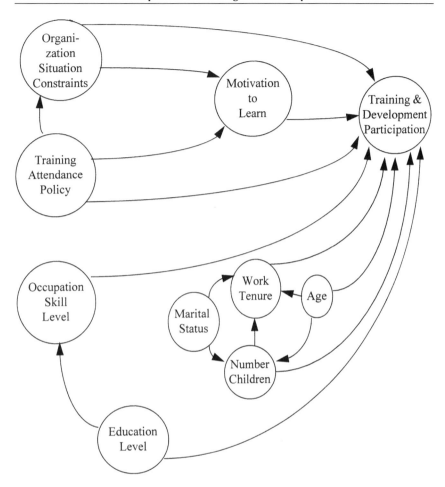

Figure 2.1 Model predicting training and development participation from selected organizational, job and personal factors

factors and human capital factors and training attitudes. For organizations to influence participation in training and development, they need to develop approaches that specifically increase the ability to attend training, including by reducing constraints on attendance and by facilitating employee benefits from training and motivation to learn. Occupation type and other job factors may still be the major impact on participation in training and development, disadvantaging groups who are under-represented at high occupation skill levels and managerial levels.

REFERENCES

Altonji, J. G. & Spletzer, J. R. (1991) Worker characteristics, job characteristics, and the receipt of on-the-job training. *Industrial and Labor Relations Review*, 45, 58–79.

Anon (1995). 1995 Industry training report. *Training*, October, 39–76.

Australian Bureau of Statistics (1992) *Labor Statistics Australia* (6101.0). Canberra: Commonwealth Government Printer.

Australian Bureau of Statistics (1993) *Employer training expenditure* (6353.0). Canberra: Commonwealth Government Printer.

Baker, M. & Wooden, M. (1992) Immigration and its impact on the incidence of training in Australia. *The Australian Economic Review*, **98**, 39–53.

Barron, J. M., Black, D. A. & Loewenstein, M. A. (1992) Gender differences in training, capital and wages. *Journal of Human Resources*, **28**, 343–363.

Bartel, A. P. (1994). Productivity gains from the implementation of employee training programs. *Industrial Relations*, **33**, 411–425.

Becker, G. S. (1975). *Human capital*. Chicago: University of Chicago Press.

Booth, A. L. (1991) Job-related formal training. *Oxford Bulletin of Economics and Statistics*, **53**, 281–294.

Booth, A. L. (1993) Private sector training and graduate earnings. *The Review of Economics and Statistics*, **75**, 164–170.

Campion, M. A., & Berger, C. J. (1990) Conceptual integration and the empirical test of job design and compensation relationships. *Personnel Psychology*, **43**, 525–553.

Cusimano, J. M. (1995) Turning blue-collar workers into knowledge workers. *Training and Development*, August, 47–49.

Dawkins, J. (1989) *Improving Australia's training system*. Canberra: Australian Government Publishing Service.

Dubin, S. S. (1990) Maintaining competence through updating. In S. S. Dubin (Ed.), *Maintaining Professional Competence* (pp. 9–45). San Francisco: Jossey-Bass.

Farr, J. L. & Middlebrooks, C. L. (1990) Enhancing motivation to participate in professional development. In S. S. Dubin (Ed.), *Maintaining Professional Competence* (1995–213). San Francisco: Jossey-Bass.

Frazis, H. J., Herz, D. E. & Horrigan, M. W. (1995) Employer-provided training: Results from a survey. *Monthly Labor Review*, May, 3–17.

Gibbins, C. (1994) Women and training. *Employment Gazette*, **11**, 391–402.

Green, F. (1991) Sex discrimination in job-related training. *British Journal of Industrial Relations*, **29**, 295–304.

Green, F. (1993) The determinants of training of male and female employees in Britain. *Oxford Bulletin of Economics and Statistics*, **55**, 103–123.

Gritz, R. M. (1993) The impact of training on the frequency and duration of employment. *Journal of Econometrics*, **57**, 21–51.

Guzzo, R. A., Jette, R. D. & Katzell, R. A. (1985) The effects of psychologically based intervention programs on worker productivity. *Personnel Psychology*, **38**, 275–292.

Hodson, R., Hooks, G. & Rieble, S. (1994) Training in the workplace: Continuity and change. *Sociological Perspectives*, **37**, 97–118.

Holden, L. (1993) European trends in training and development. *International Journal of Human Resource Management*, **2**, 113–131.

Kozlowski, S. W. J. & Farr, J. L. (1988) An integrative model of updating and performance. *Human Performance*, **1**, 5–29.

Kozlowski, S. W. J. & Hults, B. M. (1987) An exploration of climates for technical updating and performance. *Personnel Psychology*, **40**, 539–563.

Littlefield, D. (1995) Tougher training targets widespread support. *People Management*, May, 7–8.

Maurer, T. J., & Tarulli, B. A. (1994) Investigation of perceived environment, outcome and person variables in relationship to development by employees. *Journal of Applied Psychology*, **79**, 3–14.

Noe, R. A. (1996) Is career management related to employee development and performance? *Journal of Organizational Behavior*, **17**, 119–133.

Noe, R. M. & Ford, K. J. (1992) Emerging issues and new directions for training research. *Research in Personnel and Human Resources Management*, **10**, 345–384.

Noe, R. A., & Wilk, S. A. (1993) Investigation of the factors that influence employees' participation in development activities. *Journal of Applied Psychology*, **78**, 291–302.

Noe, R. A., Wilk, S. A., Mullen, E. J. & Wanek, J. E. (1996) Employee development. In J. K. Ford, S. W. J. Kozlowski, K. Kraiger, E. Salas & M. Teachout (Eds.), *Improving Training Effectiveness in Work Organizations*. Hillsdale, NJ: Erlbaum.

OECD (1993) *Industry training in Australia, Sweden and the United States*. Paris: OECD.

Phillips, S. N. (1996) Team training puts fizz in Coke plant's future. *Personnel Journal*, January, 87–92.

Rainbird, H. (1994) The changing role of the training function. *Human Resource Management Journal*, **5**, 72–90.

Robinson, A. G. & Stern, S. (1995) Strategic national HRD initiatives. *Human Resource Development Quarterly*, **6**, 123–146.

Scott, W. R. & Meyer, J. W. (1991) The rise of training programs in firms and agencies. *Research in Organizational Behavior*, **13**, 297–326.

Seibert, K. W., Hall, D. T. & Kram, K. E. (1995) Strengthening the weak link in strategic executive development. *Human Resource Management*, **34**, 549–567.

Tharenou, P. (1995) The impact of a developmental performance appraisal program on employee perceptions in an Australian federal agency. *Group and Organization Management*, **20**, 245–271.

Tharenou, P., Latimer, S. & Conroy, D. K. (1994) How do you make it to the top? An examination of influences on women's and men's managerial advancement. *Academy of Management Journal*, **37**, 899–931.

Tharenou, P. (1997b) Organizational, job and personal predictors of employee participation in training and development. *Applied Psychology: An International Review*, **46**, 112–134.

Tharenou, P. (1997a) Managerial career advancement. In C. L. Cooper and I. T. Robertson (Eds.), *International Review of Industrial and Organizational Psychology*, Vol. 12 (pp. 39–94). Chichester: Wiley.

Thatcher, M. (1995) Performance wins prizes for Pizza Hut employees. *People Management*, June, 5–6.

US Department of Labor (1989) *Investing in people*. Washington, DC: US Government Printing Service.

Veum, J. R. (1996) Gender and race differences in company training. *Industrial Relations*, **35**, 32–43.

CHAPTER 3

The Electronic Office

Thomas A. Finholt
The University of Michigan, USA

THE ELECTRONIC OFFICE

For a growing number of people, the workplace is no longer a specific physical location. Today, impromptu offices can arise anywhere and it is common for people to work at home, in public places, or while traveling. Much of this transformation is due to information technology that enables people to choose when and where they will work, without sacrificing access to staff, colleagues, and information. Some organizations are capitalizing on recent technological advances to create "electronic offices", or on-line work environments. For example, TBWA Chiat/Day, a Los Angeles-based advertising agency, has transformed their conventional office into an electronic office through the use of computer networks, fileservers, and portable computers.[1] As a result of these changes, a "day-in-the-life" of a TBWA Chiat/Day worker differs dramatically from the experience of a traditional office worker.

Upon arriving at the Los Angeles office, a TBWA Chiat/Day employee might first sit down at a desktop computer to review advertising copy marked up by a co-worker in New York. The copy is retrieved from the agency's fileserver, modified, and then saved back to the fileserver for later review by the New York employee. After completing the editing task, the Los Angeles employee moves to a conference room for a project meeting with another local worker and a client, who is joining in by video link from San Francisco. When the meeting is over, the employee grabs a laptop computer and leaves for a lunch appointment with a job candidate. The lunch goes well and it is apparent that the candidate

---

[1] To read more about TBWA Chiat/Day's transformation and corporate philosophy go to their Web page at: http://www.chiatday.com/web/index_orig.html

Trends in Organizational Behavior, Volume 4. Edited by C. L. Cooper and D. M. Rousseau.
© 1997 John Wiley & Sons Ltd.

should talk with additional TBWA Chiat/Day personnel. Consulting the firm's scheduling program, the employee quickly identifies open time slots on various workers' calendars. Finally, on the way back to the office, an email message diverts the employee to retrieve a sick child at daycare. After things are settled on the homefront, the employee logs in by modem to the agency's fileserver and finds that the colleague in New York signed off on the advertising copy changes.

The technology adopted by TBWA Chiat/Day represents an ambitious integration of off-the-shelf systems. In TBWA Chiat/Day's case, the investment required to achieve this integration was justified by clearly identified benefits. Notably, TBWA Chiat/Day workers observed that their good ideas were not confined to working hours or to the office. Therefore, technology that would allow people to do work at the beach or in a cafe, as easily as if they were at a desk at headquarters, would result in TBWA Chiat/Day capturing more of the workers' creative output. In general, organizations considering electronic office technology are concerned about the same issue confronted at TBWA Chiat/Day: Is the installation cost of electronic office systems justified in terms of increased organizational performance? Unfortunately, many organizations are poorly prepared to accurately assess the costs of creating electronic offices. Similarly, organizations are often unaware of how to identify the contribution of electronic office technology to organizational performance. As a result, organizations often stumble badly when adopting information technology and systems promoted as enhancing productivity end up creating extra work.

The irony of systems intended to save work causing more work has been labeled the "productivity paradox", and refers to the observation by Landauer (1995) that the unprecedented investment in computing technology in the US during the 1980s had no observable impact on the US gross domestic product. Landauer claims that much of the failure of this investment can be attributed to ignorance by technology developers about how users actually do their work. This chapter argues that successful adoption of technology depends on matching the functionality of potential electronic office systems to an organization's requirements, in terms of culture and work practices. At TBWA/Chiat Day, for instance, their choices fit the agency's organic, egalitarian orientation and the technology was embraced. In a more conservative organization, the same innovations might clash with cultural norms and values and be viewed with suspicion. Because matching technology to organizational requirements is difficult, the overarching theme of this chapter is understanding organizational factors that increase the probability of a favorable alignment between technology, culture, and practice. In the course of exploring this main theme, the sections that follow will summarize the capabilities of current and emerging electronic office technology, interpret real organizations' experiences with electronic office technology, and offer predictions about organizational factors correlated with the successful introduction of electronic office technology.

Capabilities of Electronic Office Technology

An electronic office is the combination of technology, software and infrastructure that allows people to work together independent of time or location. A simple definition of an electronic office might be a workplace without walls, created through the use of computers and computer networks. Development of technology to support electronic offices has not been guided by a grand plan. Rather, systems have emerged through a combination of prodding by visionary thinkers, apropriation of technology designed for other purposes, and the marketing of low-cost, high-performance personal computers. As early as 1945, Vannevar Bush proposed a global database that would allow users anywhere to access and retrieve documents. In the 1960s and 1970s, pioneering computer scientists wrote about the use of computing to support intellectual work and built prototype systems for computer-supported meetings. However, the initial practical step toward electronic offices ocurred with the opening in 1969 of the US Department of Defense's ARPAnet, the first national computer network. Although originally designed to share scarce computing resources, the most important function of the ARPAnet became its support for communication through electronic mail. Throughout the 1970s and 1980s network technologies developed further, culminating in the Internet, which in 1985 created the first worldwide computer network. Today, the US government is leading an initiative to upgrade the global information infrastructure through the construction of the so-called "information superhighway".

Four broad changes since the earliest days of the ARPAnet have created conditions conducive for electronic office development. First, electronic offices require reliable and cheap access to international and national computer networks. When the ARPAnet appeared its bandwidth was limited and network use was restricted to those organizations with ARPA projects, primarily universities and defense contractors. Today, network use has expanded dramatically and it is common for commercial organizations as well as private individuals to purchase network access through Internet service providers, such as America Online or CompuServe. Second, electronic offices require reliable local area networks. In the early days, network connections were scarce, often limited to one or two machines per organization. Today, because of the proliferation of local area network technology connections are ubiquitous, akin to telephone jacks. Third, electronic offices require software that is easy to use and can be learned quickly. Early software had arcane user interfaces. Today, most software products have intuitive, graphical interfaces, such as the Macintosh operating system, that allow users to perform sophisticated actions without learning obscure command sequences. Finally, electronic offices require equipment that can go where people need to go to do their work. In the beginning of the computer era, computers were room-sized machines operated in carefully controlled environments. Today, computers are the size of notebooks, have no special operating requirements, and offer performance thousands of times better than mainframe computers of the past.

At a more specific level, electronic offices must allow people to use the infrastructure described above to collaborate. Twenty years of research have led to a rich variety of tools for the support of collaborative work. Combinations of these tools, along with the infrastructure described above, form the core capabilities that constitute an electronic office. As shown in Figure 3.1, the capabilities of an electronic office consist of technology to link people with people, technology to link people with information, and technology to link people with facilities—all integrated through computer networks.

The TBWA Chiat/Day example described a number of people-to-people technologies, including: (a) fileservers, or the use of computer networks to share access to a common computer file or group of files; (b)

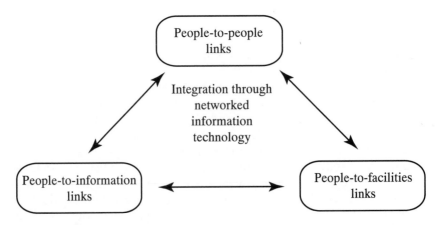

Figure 3.1 The electronic office uses networked information technology to create people-to-people, people-to-information, and people-to-facilities links.

videoconferencing, or the use of computer networks and software to transmit and receive live video images; and (c) electronic mail (email), or the use of computers and computer networks to store and forward messages. Other instances of people-to-people technology include shared editors, where writers can work together to produce and revise a text online, and tools to reproduce in an online environment the social cues that are normally available only in a shared physical setting, such as the use of "open" or "closed" office door icons to signal availability.

The TBWA Chiat/Day example illustrated one kind of people-to-information technology, in the form of the scheduling program, which tracked individual calendars and resolved schedule conflicts. Other instances of people-to-information technology include the World Wide Web (the Web), an *ad hoc* system for classifying data on individual computers that makes this information searchable and retrievable through the Internet. Graphically oriented applications for searching the Web, called "browsers", have gained broad acceptance, and several, such as Netscape Navigator® and Microsoft Internet Explorer®, have become among the most popular computer applications ever written.

Finally, technologies to link people with facilities include the ability to directly control remote equipment For example, animators at TBWA Chiat/Day might use their computer network access to buy time on a supercomputer to orchestrate the composition of a digitally rendered image. Other instances of people-to-facilities technology might range from monitoring the status of a manufacturing process at a remote factory to checking a weather radar at a travel destination to see if flights will be delayed.

EXPERIENCES WITH ELECTRONIC OFFICE TECHNOLOGIES

People-to-People Technology

The phenomenon of the electronic office is so recent that there is very little empirical data on organizations' experiences with integrated electronic office systems. However, the individual technologies that make up an electronic office have been in use by some organizations for several years. This section summarizes the results of research on organizations using people-to-people technology.

Fileservers

An emerging use of fileservers is to support group or organizational databases. These databases may be used to record and report progress among distributed workers, to accumulate shared documents, or to save ongoing conversations. The most well-known group database application is Notes®, produced by Lotus Development. A number of case studies of Notes use have been written. Orlikowski (1992) examined the use of Notes at an accounting firm. In this firm the top management made a public and costly commitment to Notes. The hope was that Notes would improve information sharing among partners and associates, and in this fashion allow the firm to better exploit employees' expertise to meet clients' needs. In practice, the Notes implementation was a spectacular failure. First, within the billing system of the firm, there was no mechanism to compensate employees for time spent reading or generating Notes content. Second, among the associates, the competition for partnerships made them loath to share information that might create an advantage for another associate.

Olson and Teasley (1996) studied the use of Notes by members of a geographically distributed design team in the engineering division of an auto manufacturer. Within the team, the members adopted Notes to record and track action items for attention by other team members. The team enthusiastically used Notes over a period of several months. However, Notes fell into disuse for several reasons. First, the use of Notes made members' progress too visible to the team's manager. Second, it proved too time consuming to enter and track items in Notes, compared to simply performing the tasks or delegating responsibility face-to-face. Finally, while the team manager used Notes to track the team's progress, the manager did not personally enter any information into the Notes database. This led the team to think that the manager did not value use of the Notes system, despite the fact that the manager was actively reading contributions by team members.

Videoconferences

Videoconferences have been used for some time, but the high cost of maintaining special rooms and connections traditionally limited their utility. The recent development of desktop videoconference technology, such as Cornell University's CU-SeeMe and Intel's ProShare® means that ordinary users are now able to conduct videoconferences using inexpensive off-the-shelf equipment over the Internet. Anticipating the emergence of desktop videoconference technology, a number of research and development labs have experimented with ubiquitous video links, or entire work groups that are connected to videoconference systems. These experiments have taken two forms. In one form, remote facilities were connected with a continuous video connection, often placed in a commons room or lounge. The expectation was that the continuous video connection would simulate, across distances, the kind of spontaneous encounters that occur when workers are co-located. Unfortunately, experiences at Xerox's Palo Alto Research Center (Abel, 1990) suggested that limitations of the technology placed too many constraints on interaction. For example, users were unable to make eye-to-eye contact over the video link. Further, poor resolution made it difficult to share views of drawings and documents. Finally, delays in audio and video signals meant that conversations often had a disjointed quality that impaired natural discourse. In the second kind of video experiment, individual users were connected to a video switch that allowed them to "glance" at other users to determine their availability to meet or talk, much as co-located workers might stick their heads into each other's offices when going to lunch. Experience with this kind of video technology proved more satisfactory than the continuous video connections, although video-mediated conversations still required more effort than face-to-face conversations. For example, Fish et al. (1992) found that mentors and mentees on opposite sides of a research facility were able to use video links to monitor one another. Similarly, Tang & Rua (1994) found that the use of video links led to spontaneous and informal interaction among geographically distributed workers.

Email

Email is a form of computer-mediated communication where people can exchange messages containing text and graphics via national and international computer networks. Email is fast compared with postal mail, it can be addressed to a single recipient as easily as to a large group, and email messages can be read or reread at any time. Email is perhaps the most widespread electronic office technology in use today. Kiesler and Sproull (1991) summarize a systematic program of sociological and psychological research on organizational email use conducted by their group at Carnegie Mellon University. Three key findings emerged from the field studies done by the Carnegie Mellon group. First, the use of email reduces social context. For example the text-based nature of email attenuates context information, such as status cues, in ways that can reduce barriers to participation in work group discussions by lower-status workers. Second, email allows workers to create electronic groups through email mailing lists. Analysis of electronic groups shows that they exhibit many of the characteristics of face-to-face groups, such as decision making and norm formation, while often consisting of hundreds of members at dozens of locations. Finally, email allows workers to identify and make contact with like-minded others, despite geographic or temporal barriers. For example, in one study, nightshift workers used email to stay current with the activities of the majority of their co-workers, who were on the day-shift.

People-to-information Technologies

The evolution of people-to-information technologies is occurring rapidly. Much of this development has been spurred by the explosive growth in use of the World Wide Web. In the future, systems like the Web can be expected to become more specialized and more searchable. In this sense, data on use of digital archives may be predictive of future use of the Web. Similarly, experience with search aids, like social information filtering, may offer insight into how users may better retrieve information from the Web.

Digital Archives

As noted above, email is a good way for like-minded people to share information, despite geographic and temporal barriers. For example, in some organizations, email mailing lists are used to assist workers in seeking help from others. Yet, much of the potential of mailing lists for seeking help is lost because of the ephemeral nature of email list conversations. In recognition of this many organizations have created digital archives, or online collections of messages sent over mailing lists. An advantage of digital archives is that archive users can access mailing list information without having been original recipients on the mailing list. In some sense, digital archives represent a new kind of organizational memory consisting of shared know-how, rather than formal records. In a study of digital archives used by field engineers in an international computer company, Finholt (1997) found interesting differences in archive use depending on the extent to which archives facilitated the sharing of know-how. One archive, called Colleague, consisted of messages exchanged over a company-wide mailing list addressed to all field engineers. The other archive, called Expert, was a collection of messages exchanged between individual engineers and designated experts. The chief difference between the two archives was that Colleague more closely mimicked the features of co-location that facilitate sharing of know-how, such as providing awareness of helpful contacts and information about "who knows what". Analyses of use showed that engineers used Colleague more than Expert and that combined archive use increased with greater geographic remoteness from knowledgeable colleagues. Also, greater geographic remoteness tended to increase use of Colleague more than use of Expert.

Social Information Filtering Technology

There is widespread recognition that much of the potential value of a resource like the Web is untapped because people can't find needed information. One approach to solving this problem has focused on aggregating the shared search experiences of many users to reveal mutually useful paths to information. This process, termed "social information filtering," assumes that the effort to identify useful content amidst complex and poorly organized collections of information can be dramatically reduced through hints from others who have searched through the same information. Social information filtering technology (SIFT) can help users "sift" through layers of information by directly or indirectly applying the experience of others who have "sifted" through the same information seeking similar content. In a test of the SIFT concept, Ackerman (1994) built a system called Answer Garden and tested it within a group of astrophysicists. Answer Garden was designed to make recorded information retrievable and to make knowledgeable others accessible. In use, queries from Answer Garden users are first directed to the archived contents of the system. If a query matches archived content, then the stored information is provided to the question-asker. In the event that a question does not match an existing stored answer, then the system forwards the question through a cascading chain of expert answerers. The contents of questions and answers resolved through this chain are accumulated in a database. In cases where the chain of experts fails to resolve a question, experts can offer recommendations for referrals and these data are also encoded into the database to build up inferences to direct future queries. Observing use of Answer Garden by the astrophysicists, Ackerman identified two strengths. First, the iterative accumulation of information in the system's database gave users feedback to: correct poorly formed questions; ask follow-up questions; and to recommend changes in the indexing structure of the database. Second, Answer Garden allowed for production of information on demand, therefore the system grew where users needed information the most and helped expert respondents direct their expertise where others needed it the most.

People-to-facilities Technology

Not all electronic offices include technology to support links between people and facilities. But in many situations, such links may be critical. For example, a highly touted application area is telemedicine, where specialists can conduct exams or tests of patients at remote clinics. The National Research Council (1993) has identified the development of better technologies for remotely controlling equipment and instruments as a crucial research goal for the early twenty-first century.

Collaboratories

One place where electronic office technology has come together to support collaborative work is in the scientific arena giving birth to a new kind of organization, dubbed a "collaboratory" (Finholt & Olson, 1997). A collaboratory is an online laboratory where distant colleagues can interact with one another, use instruments, and share data. For example, the Upper Atmospheric Research Collaboratory (UARC) supports an international community of space physicists by providing them with real-time control of instruments at an observatory in Greenland, the ability to communicate with their colleagues about shared real-time data, and access to archived data. In UARC, a half dozen instruments in Greenland transmit data over the Internet to specially designed display programs. Scientists at ten sites around the world can view these displays simultaneously by running the data viewing programs on local machines. A simple text-based "chat" window allows the scientists to share reactions with each other about the phenomena they are observing and change the settings of the observatory instruments. Simple collaboration support, such as the ability to mark notable data, share common views of data streams, and point to data features, is also provided to assist real-time interactions. Among other things, use of UARC has significantly reduced barriers to conducting experiments using the Greenland instruments. Pre-UARC, scientists traveled to Greenland and often had to schedule long visits to ensure that they would achieve optimal data collection conditions at least once. With UARC, scientists can monitor conditions in Greenland from their home laboratories and are able to more easily capitalize on good data gathering conditions as well as to continue other work if conditions are bad.

Organizational Factors Correlated with Successful Introduction of Electronic Office Technology

The previous section reviewed empirical observations of organizations' experiences with technologies that will constitute core capabilities of electronic offices. From these studies of individual technologies it is possible to identify a list of organizational factors that may correlate positively with successful adoption of electronic office systems.

First, electronic office technology has the potential to reduce the costs of spanning geographic and organizational boundaries. In organizations where increased boundary-spanning is framed as an opportunity rather than a threat, workers will be free to use electronic office systems to exercise initiative in seeking and sharing expertise, with likely gains for the organization. For example, Hutchins (1995) has suggested that unhindered access by workers to organization-wide information systems might improve the efficiency of organizational information retrieval, with corresponding competitive advantages relative to organizations with less liberal information system use policies.

Second, electronic office technology has the potential to create new tasks and new job categories. In organizations that recognize and reward new ways of working made possible through electronic office systems, workers will use electronic offices to share information and collaborate, with likely benefits for the organization. For instance, in the company studied by Finholt, authors of particularly useful contributions to the digital archives were often recognized with awards and promotions, which encouraged a steady stream of contributions to the archives. However, where organizations fail to match incentives with new ways of working, as in the accounting firm described by Orlikowski, the full capabilities of electronic offices will be underutilized or ignored.

Finally, electronic office technology has the potential to generate new obligations for workers, without necessarily relieving existing obligations. In organizations that allow electronic office work to replace traditional office work, workers will embrace electronic office systems. But, if use of electronic office technology is seen as an additional burden, workers will reject the technology. For example, in the case described by Olson and Teasley, the engineers stopped using Notes because they thought the system was redundant with more conventional technologies, such as the telephone, and they thought management was ignoring the Notes contributions. Similarly, early studies of telework showed dissatisfaction as women working at home found themselves unable to disentangle their jobs from duties as caregivers and housekeepers.

In addition to these organizational factors, there are factors inherent in electronic office technology that may limit its success. Specifically, desktop video links may never achieve the same quality as face-to-face conversation at affordable rates, and sensitivity to this difference may bias organizations toward in-person meetings rather than video-mediated meetings. Similarly, while progress has been made in the design of user interfaces to operating systems, the evolution of systems is still rapid enough to mean that a typical worker might need to learn several systems over the course of a career. Finally, the growth in Internet use is pushing the limits of the underlying *circa*-1985 (and earlier) technology. As a result, applications like collaboratories may never receive widespread acceptance because lags and delays due to worldwide network congestion make these applications too cumbersome and slow for practical use.

An appropriate closing thought might be to observe that gains from the use of electronic office systems are likely, but features of organizations and of electronic office technology do not make these gains automatic. To return to Landauer's point, much of the success of electronic offices will depend on whether developers can incorporate understandings about work that organizations put into the design of electronic offices. In this regard, people who study organizations, both practitioners and scholars, will need to become actively engaged in thinking about the design of electronic office technology. One strategy that shows promise suggests that electronic office technology should evolve according to principles of user-centered design. That is, unlike the past where designers and users were independent of one another, in the future, designers and users will need to form a productive dialog, where user feedback helps designers to better tailor and enhance systems.

SUMMARY

Information technologies are transforming when and where work occurs. For the first time it is possible to imagine workplaces without walls, or electronic offices. This chapter describes the core technologies that constitute electronic office systems as well as organizations' experiences with these technologies. A key conclusion is that organizational gains through the adoption of electronic offices are possible, but not automatic. Specifically, the success of electronic offices will depend on how organizations respond to potential changes introduced by electronic office technology, including expanded opportunities for boundary-spanning, new ways of working, and the creation of additional work-related obligations.

ACKNOWLEDGEMENT

I am grateful for helpful comments on earlier versions by Stephanie Teasley.

NOTE

Requests for pre-prints should be addressed to (a) finholt @ umich.edu or (b) Thomas A. Finholt, CREW, 701 Tappan St, Ann Arbor, MI 48109-1234, USA.

REFERENCES

Abel, M. (1990) Experiences in an exploratory distributed organization. In J. Galegher, R. E. Kraut, and C. Egido (Eds.), *Intellectual teamwork: Foundations of cooperative work* (pp. 489–510). Hillsdale, NJ: Lawrence Erlbaum Associates.

Ackerman, M. S. (1994) Augmenting the organizational memory: A field study of Answer Garden. In *Proceedings of the ACM Conference on Computer supported Cooperative Work*, pp. 243–252. New York: ACM Press.

Bush, V. (1945) As we may think. *The Atlantic Monthly*, **176**, 101–108.

Finholt, T. A. (1997) Outsiders on the inside: Sharing know-how through computer message archives. Manuscript submitted for publication.

Finholt, T. A. & Olson, G. M. (in press) From laboratories to collaboratories: A new organizational form for scientific collaboration. Forthcoming in *Psychological Science*.

Fish, R. S., Kraut, R. E., Root, R. W. & Rice, R. E. (1992) Evaluating video as a technology for informal communication. In *Proceedings of the ACM Conference on Human Factors in Computing Systems*, pp. 37–48. New York: ACM Press.

Hutchins, E. (1995) *Cognition in the wild*. Cambridge, MA: MIT Press.

Kiesler, S. & Sproull, L. S. (1991) *Connections: New ways of working in the networked organization*. Cambridge, MA: MIT Press.

Landauer, T. (1995) *The Trouble with Computers: Usefulness, Usability, and Productivity*. Cambridge, MA: MIT Press.

Olson, J. S. & Teasley, S. D. (1996) Groupware in the wild: Lessons learned from a year of virtual colocation. In *Proceedings of the ACM Conference on Computer Supported Work 1996*, Cambridge, MA, pp. 419–427.

Orlikowski, W. (1992) Learning from Notes: Organizational issues in groupware implementation. In *Proceedings of the ACM Conference on Computer Supported Work 1992*, pp. 362–369. New York: ACM Press.

National Research Council (1993) *National Collaboratories: Applying Information Technology for Scientific Research*. Washington, D.C.: National Academy Press.

Tang, J. & Rua, M. (1994) Montage: Providing teleproximity for distributed groups. In *Proceedings of the ACM Conference on Human Factors in Computing Systems*, pp. 37–43. New York: ACM Press.

CHAPTER 4

A Relative Deprivation Approach to Understanding Underemployment

Daniel C. Feldman
University of South Carolina

Carrie R. Leana
University of Pittsburgh

and

William H. Turnley
University of South Carolina

A RELATIVE DEPRIVATION APPROACH TO UNDERSTANDING UNDEREMPLOYMENT

Relative deprivation theory has long been used to understand how individuals react to situations of frustrated expectations. Since Stouffer's pioneering work on feelings of relative deprivation among soliders (Stouffer et al, 1949), social psychologists have been investigating such issues as whether relative deprivation stems from negative reactions to past experiences or thwarted expectations about the future, why subjective feelings of relative deprivation often do not correspond to "objective" distributions of outcomes, whom people take as their comparative other in making assessments of relative deprivation, and when individuals are likely to believe their relative deprivation is based on their own personal (or "egoistic") circumstances rather than their group (or "fraternal") membership.

Most of the research on relative deprivation in psychology has

Trends in Organizational Behavior, Volume 4. Edited by C. L. Cooper and D. M. Rousseau.
© 1997 John Wiley & Sons Ltd.

examined such social problems as gender and racial inequality. For example, Stouffer's work examined why black soldiers who were stationed in the southern US during World War II experienced less relative deprivation than did those stationed in northern facilities. Similarly, Crosby's pioneering work (1982, 1984) has examined such paradoxes as why working women—despite their awareness of sex discrimination—feel relatively little sense of personal deprivation. To the extent that the theory has been employed to examine organizational or work-related issues, it has been used to examine feelings of relative deprivation regarding compensation and whom employees use as comparative others in assessing relative deprivation in terms of pay (e.g., Martin, 1981; Oldham et al, 1986).

In this paper, we use relative deprivation theory to examine underemployment. While precise figures on the extent of underemployment are not readily available, the figure of 25% of the US workforce being underemployed seems to be a reasonable estimate (Henry, 1994; Newman, 1993). Three groups of workers, in particular, appear to be highly represented in the underemployed category: laid-off workers re-employed in lower-paying, less demanding jobs (Leana & Feldman, 1995); part-time and temporary workers involuntarily employed in contingent work (Tilly, 1991); and new college graduates holding jobs which do not require as much education as they possess (Feldman & Turnley, 1995; Winefield et al, 1991).

In this paper we utilize relative deprivation theory to inform our understanding of underemployment and to untangle previously inconsistent or inconclusive research in the area. By examining such issues as the conditions leading to relative deprivation, the choice of "referent others", and factors which mitigate or exacerbate relative deprivation, we can better understand how people define themselves as being underemployed and under what circumstances they experience the greatest sense of frustration.

Underemployment Research

While definitions of underemployment vary both between and within academic disciplines, all share two key elements. First, underemployment is defined as an inferior, lesser, or lower quality of employment (Kaufman, 1982). Second, underemployment is defined relative to some standard of comparison. In some cases, underemployment is defined relative to the employment experiences of others with the same education and work history (e.g. Quinn & Mandilovitch, 1975). For example, some researchers define underemployment in terms of having more formal education, higher-level skills, or more extensive work experience than the job requires. In other cases, underemployment is defined relative to the person's own past education and work history (e.g., Borgen, Amundson, & Harder, 1988). For instance, some researchers have conceptualized underemployment in terms of involuntary contingent employment or the wage differential between individuals' current jobs and their last positions (e.g., Feldman & Turnley, 1995). In each definition, however, underemployment is specified in terms of its relative disadvantage to other forms of employment.

Analogous to relative deprivation researchers, those who study underemployment agree that it, too, it based on both objective experiences and subjective interpretations of those experiences. Moreover, most research suggests that there are degrees of underemployment (i.e., that underemployment is not a dichotomous variable) and that underemployment has consequences for individuals' cognitions, affective reactions, and behaviors.

Because underemployment is an important labor utilization issue, there has been some research on the negative consequences with which it might be highly associated. Underemployment has been consistently linked with poorer job satisfaction, job involvement, and relationships with co-workers (Borgen, Amundson & Harder, 1988; Khan & Morrow, 1991), and more generally with poorer overall mental health (Winefield et al., 1991). In addition, underemployment has been linked to more negative attitudes towards one's career (Burris, 1983; Feldman & Turnley, 1995). At the level of job behaviors, underemployment seems to be most closely linked to higher turnover (Feldman, Doerpinghaus, & Turnley, 1995; Robinson, Kraatz, & Rousseau, 1994) and less energetic or focused job performance (Burris, 1983).

One particularly interesting research stream on the consequences of underemployment has examined the relative sense of dissatisfaction experienced by underemployed workers and unemployed workers. On the one hand, Jahoda (1982) has argued that any employment, even underemployment, is preferable to no employment because of the "latent" functions" jobs provide: increased social interactions at work, a greater sense of personal identity, and greater structure to the day. However, other researchers have found that underemployed workers are psychologically worse off than the unemployed because they have given up hope of finding a good job (Leana & Feldman, 1995).

Despite the importance of underemployment as an employment issue today, relatively little theoretical work has informed the modest amount of empirical research on the topic. In the next section, we discuss relative deprivation theory and how it can inform how underemployment is conceptualized in theory, experienced by workers, and measured in future research.

Relative Deprivation Theory

Crosby's original work on relative deprivation (1976) suggested that there were five preconditions for individuals to experience relative deprivation: (1) they want some object X; (2) they feel entitled to X; (3) they perceive that someone else possesses X; (4) they think it feasible to attain X; and (5) they refuse personal responsibility for their current failure to possess X themselves. In subsequent refinements of her theory, Crosby (1984) simplify her model to focus on two basic preconditions: (1) wanting X, and (2) deserving X. Along similar lines, Martin (1981) writes that relative deprivation stems from a comparison between the rewards received by one's self or one's group and the rewards received by some other person or group. Most researchers in the area, then, agreee that relative deprivation derives from (1) wanting some outcome, (2) feeling deserving of that outcome, (3) not receiving that outcome, and (4) perceiving that some comparative other receives the desired outcome or more of the desired outcome.

The research on relative deprivation has examined three issues in particular: (1) the referent others that individuals use to assess relative deprivation, (2) the degree of relative deprivation individuals experience, and (3) the mitigating or exacerbating circumstances that influence the amount of relative deprivation experienced.

Choice of Referent Others

Certainly a key element in the research on relative deprivation has been the choice of comparison others. This research has focused on several different issues. First, some researchers have examined whom individuals take as their referent others. Comparisons may be made in several ways: "similar up" (comparisons to people who are basically in the same circumstances but receive more valued outcomes), "similar down", "dissimilar up" (comparisons to people who are basically in different circumstances but receive more valued outcomes), or "dissimilar down". Because people have strong preferences for comparisons to similar others and comparisons to those who are better off, the research suggests that individuals are most likely to compare themselves "similar up", followed by "dissimilar up", "similar down", and "dissimilar down" (Martin, 1981).

Second, individuals use multiple comparison others in assessing the fairness of outcomes (Dornstein, 1989). Moreover, people use multiple dimensions of similarity/dissimilarity in making comparisons. Thus, individuals may use various dimensions such as gender, age, race, job tenure, and perceived competencies in assessing their outcomes relative to others (Ambrose & Kulik, 1988; Goodman, 1974).

Third, there has been considerable research on the issue of "egoistic" vs. "fraternal" relative deprivation, namely, whether individuals compare their own situation to that of other individuals (egoistic deprivation) or whether individuals compare the situation of their group as a whole to that of other groups (fraternal deprivation). This research stream suggests that egoistic deprivation occurs more frequently than fraternal deprivation. Crosby (1984) argues that this is because people are disinclined to assert group victimization or to look for villains. Whether this finding would be as true in today's culture, particularly as applied to the state of underemployment, is unclear. Another consistent research finding here is that while egoistic deprivation is closely tied to emotional reactions, fraternal deprivation is more closely tied to voice or protest behaviors (Guimond & Dubé-Simard, 1983).

Degree of Relative Deprivation

A second stream of research on relative deprivation has examined the circumstances under which individuals experience the most relative deprivation. Almost all researchers in the area agreee that relative deprivation is based on both objective experiences and subjective interpretations of those experiences, and that relative deprivation is not a dichotomous variable but rather is experienced in degrees.

Several factors contribute to the experienced degree of relative deprivation. One is the distance between the outcomes an individual receives and the outcomes the individual expects; the greater the distance the greater the sense of relative deprivation. A second is the similarity of the comparison other. The greater the similarity between an individual and his/her comparative other, the more likely the individual is to experience outcome differences as relative deprivation, since reasonable explanations or justifications for the differences in outcomes are less likely. A third, and related, factor is the attributions individuals make about the reasons for the differences in their outcomes from those of comparative others. If individuals blame themselves for their lower outcomes, they will experience less relative deprivation than if they blame external events.

Another key factor in understanding the degree of relative deprivation is the extent to which individuals feel a sense of entitlement to future rewards. The greater the sense of entitlement to future outcomes, the greater the sense of relative deprivation individuals will experience. Along similar lines, Folger and his colleagues have argued that relative deprivation will be greater when individuals can easily envision an alternative algorithm for distributing rewards under which they would be more likely to prosper (cf. Folger & Martin, 1986). In their work on referent cognition theory, Folger and his colleagues found that resentment is greater when individuals perceive the distribution procedures as unfair and when alternative procedures would have led to their receiving better outcomes.

Mitigating/Exacerbating Circumstances

The third stream of research on relative deprivation examines the circumstances that heighten or ameliorate the amount of relative deprivation individuals experience. In general, this research has drawn heavily on the literatures on procedural and distributive justice (Bies, 1987; Greenberg, 1987). Along with the work of Folger and his colleagues, this work suggests that individuals will experience different levels of relative deprivation depending upon how outcomes were distributed and the perceived fairness of the outcome distribution itself.

For example, Bies (1987) argued that the severity of experienced injustice (and, by extension, the degree of experienced relative deprivation) will be greater: (a) the more apparent responsibility the harmdoer has for the adverse action or outcome; and (b) the fewer justifications, excuses, or apologies the harmdoer offers for his/her actions. Researchers such as Cropanzano (1993) suggest, as well, that the procedures used to distribute rewards can mitigate or exacerbate relative deprivation; the more the procedures for distributive rewards are perceived as unfair, the greater the sense of relative deprivation. In most cases, though, the empirical evidence suggests that the actual value of the outcomes influences whether an outcome is perceived as fair or not. That is, individuals are more likely to perceive the distribution procedures as unfair if they themselves do relatively poorly in terms of receiving outcomes (Greenberg, 1987).

Underemployment and Relative Deprivation

By any definition, underemployment is a state where rewards or desired outcomes are not as available as they might be. Thus, relative deprivation theory may inform the research on underemployment and suggest avenues for future investigation. Paralleling our earlier treatment of relative deprivation theory, we discuss below three issues in particular regarding underemployment: (1) the choice of referent other in determining the state of underemployment; (2) the degree of relative deprivation experienced by those defined as underemployed; and (3) mitigating or exacerbating circumstances influencing the amount of relative deprivation experienced.

Choice of Referent Others

The employment circumstances of individuals should affect whom they compare themselves to in determining perceived underemployment. Relative deprivation theory, as well as social identity theory, suggests that individuals seek out similar others in making comparisons about their outcomes. In the case of laid-off workers, those similar others are likely to be co-workers not laid off. Indeed, research on both how laid-off workers react to unemployment (Leana & Feldman, 1992) and how "survivors" react to layoffs in their organizations (Brockner, 1990) suggests that workers compare the qualifications of laid-off workers to those of survivors in assessing the justice of the choice of layoff targets.

In contrast, contingent workers are more likely to use permanent employees in comparable jobs in assessing relative deprivation. Since contingent workers spend a great deal of time interacting with employees in comparable permanent jobs and have more knowledge about their relative qualifications and financial rewards, permanent employees are their most likely referent others. In empirical research on perceived pay equity, Feldman, Doerpinghaus & Turnley (1995) found contingent workers were significantly more likely to use permanent employees in the same organization as their referent others rather than contingent employees in comparable jobs in other firms. Along similar lines, we would expect underemployed college graduates to use their better-employed classmates as comparative others, both because of similarities in background and because of their better knowledge of their peers' relative qualifications and rewards.

This suggests the following set of propositions:

1A. In assessing their relative deprivation, laid-off workers will use "survivors" who were not laid off as their primary referent others.
1B. In assessing their relative deprivation, contingent workers will use permanent employees in comparable jobs with their present employers as their primary referent others.
1C. In assessing their relative deprivation, underemployed college graduates will use classmates employed in better jobs as their primary referent others.

As noted by other researchers, assessing relative deprivation is seldom a simple process and many individuals use multiple comparison others in assessing the fairness of outcomes. With regard to underemployment, individuals who have held a greater number of previous jobs and worked for more organizations are likely to know more comparable others and to use a greater variety of referent others in assessing relative deprivation. A new college graduate who is underemployed has few readily available comparison others besides his/her close schoolmates; in contrast, laid-off workers with twenty or thirty years experience in the labor market may have many others.

The work of self-categorization theorists suggests that members of groups which have historically experienced discrimination are more likely to define themselves in terms of group membership (Turner et al., 1994). Consequently, when women, minorities, or older workers find themselves underemployed, they are more likely to seek out information on whether their demographic group members are disproportionately represented in the same predicament. For these individuals, then, demographic group membership may be as salient as work group membership.

Using relative deprivation theory here may be helpful in illuminating the wide variance in research results in how people react to underemployment. While the objective amount of deprivation may be similar across underemployed individuals, their subjective assessments may vary dramatically, because of both the number of referent others they use and the diversity of internal and external referents used. The following propositions are suggested:

2A. The greater the number of previous jobs and previous employers, the more referent others underemployed workers will use in assessing relative deprivation.

2B. Women, minorities, and older workers are more likely to use demographic group referents than males, Caucasians, and younger workers.

While "egoistic" relative deprivation is generally more common than "fraternal" relative deprivation, women, minorities, and older workers are more likely to experience "fraternal" relative deprivation. Both because of public attention to discrimination issues and because of enactment of legislation protecting these groups, women, minorities, and older workers may have heightened attention to workplace decisions which adversely affect them as a group. For example, research on contingent workers suggests that women are disproportionately represented in contingent jobs (Tilly, 1991) and that older workers may be disproportionately represented in layoffs (Langley, 1984). It is not surprising, then, that these workers would have a greater sense of fraternal deprivation.

Moreover, because of this sense of fraternal deprivation, members of these groups are more likely to formally protest and litigate when forced into underemployment. Consistent with relative deprivation theory, fraternal deprivation is predicted to be more highly associated than egoistic deprivation with protest behaviors. Thus, in the case of layoffs, we would expect these groups to be more likely to litigate, both because of the salience of their group membership and because of the availability of class action lawsuits as a possible recourse (Langley, 1984). A similar picture emerges with female and minority contingent workers, who are more likely to formally protest their relative lack of benefits and relative lack of progression into full-time jobs compared to their white, male counterparts (Feldman, Doerpinghaus & Turnley, 1995). This research, then, suggests the following propositions:

3A. Women, minorities, and older workers are more likely to experience "fraternal" relative deprivation.
3B. Women, minorities, and older workers are more likely to formally protest and litigate when underemployed.

As noted earlier, underemployment has been defined in a variety of ways by scholars. In some cases, underemployment is defined relative to others in comparable situations; in other cases, underemployment is defined relative to the individual's own personal circumstances. When the difference in outcomes between the individual's present job and either the immediately preceding one or the hoped-for next job is very high, the individual will be more likely to use self-referents in assessing deprivation.

The rationale here is that large contrast effects between one's own internal desires and objective outcomes may focus underemployed individuals' attention internally. If someone experiences an objectively steep drop in pay (e.g., a laid-off worker making only 75% of his former wages in a replacement job) or a bitter disappointment in terms of reaching his aspiration (e.g., a new college graduate making $5.00/hour at Wal-Mart), the fact that many of his peers also have low paying jobs or even no jobs at all will be less salient to him. In other words, as the following propositions suggest, the greater the objective deprivation relative to the person's expected career path, the smaller the role social comparisons will play in subjective assessments:

4A. The greater the difference in outcomes between the individual's present job and the immediately preceding one, the more likely an individual is to use self-referents.

4B. The greater the difference in outcomes between the individual's present job and his/her level of aspiration, the more likely an individual is to use self-referents.

Degree of Relative Deprivation

Kelly's attribution theory (1973) suggests that individuals try to cognitively explain or make sense of aversive actions which happen to them. If individuals can attribute the reason for their bad outcomes to external events outside their control, they are more likely to experience relative deprivation (Crosby, 1976, 1984). The relative deprivation comes in part from feeling randomly or unfairly disadvantaged. In contrast, if underemployed workers take personal responsibility for their predicaments, they are less likely to feel relative deprivation. In this scenario, the individuals' predicaments are due to their own behavior (or lack thereof) rather than to some external or random factors. In essence, then, while their outcomes are poor, those outcomes are at least seen as somewhat fair.

In the context of underemployment, workers who feel their underemployment is due to their own performance will be less likely to experience relative deprivation than those who attribute their predicament to external forces. Thus, while laid-off workers who lose their jobs due to their own poor performance may be more depressed (Leana & Feldman, 1992), they will experience less relative deprivation since the layoff is not totally unfair.

On the other hand, individuals who become underemployed because of large-scale downsizings or due to recessions, economic downturns, or industry-wide reverses are more likely to experience relative deprivation. As the next two propositions suggest, when corporate-level actions, macroeconomic trends or industry sector trends are largely accountable for poor employment prospects, individuals are likely both to feel pessimistic about their chances of receiving better jobs and to experience more relative deprivation. The source of their underemployment is external, and their chances of reversing the underemployment, even if they exert substantial effort, are low.

5A. Individuals who perceive they are underemployed due to their own performance are likely to experience less relative deprivation than those who attribute their predicament to external forces.

5B. Individuals who become underemployed during large-scale downsizings, widespread economic downturns, or industry-wide reverses are likely to experience more relative deprivation.

As noted earlier, most conceptualizations of underemployment include both elements of "wanting" an outcome and "deserving" that outcome. In other words, relative deprivation stems not only from the thwarting of some desire but also from a sense of entitlement to some reward.

Underemployed white-collar workers typically report more relative deprivation than blue-collar workers (Newman, 1993). Compared to blue-collar workers, underemployed white-collar workers may experience more loss of income and job security (Leana & Feldman, 1992, 1995); thus, in terms of *objective* amounts of rewards, white-collar workers may experience a greater drop than blue-collar workers. Moreover, white-collar workers generally feel a greater sense of entitlement to those outcomes. In part, this sense of entitlement comes from greater investment in formal education; in part, this sense of entitlement comes from long-standing corporate norms about job security for managers, only opened to question this decade. In contrast, blue-collar workers have historically had little job security and, as a group, have experienced layoffs and underemployment more frequently. While additional periods of underemployment are still unsettling, they are neither out of the ordinary nor totally unexpected.

Mid-career employees may also be likely to experience greater relative deprivation than individuals at other career stages. Returning to Kelly's attribution theory (1973), individuals in mid-career are likely to experience their underemployment most intensely and to view their predicament as most irreversible. Mid-career employees experience their underemployment most intensely because they have invested heavily in their jobs and feel entitled to continued rewards. In addition, they are at the peak of their heaviest expense years with mortgages and college tuition for their children, so any drop in income or job security is highly salient (Dunn, 1979). Moreover, mid-career employees may be more pessimistic about reversing their underemployment due to age discrimination in the market place and because of their aversion to retraining or relocation in order to obtain more satisfactory employment (Dyer, 1973). By way of comparison, early-career employees are likely to view their predicament as more easily reversible, while late-career employees are likely to view their predicament as less intense, both because their high-expense years are past and because the time until retirement and the receipt of private and government pensions is closer. This research suggests the following two propositions:

6A. Underemployed white-collar workers will experience greater relative deprivation than will underemployed blue-collar workers.

6B. Relative to individuals in other career stages, mid-career underemployed workers will experience more relative deprivation.

As noted earlier, there has been much debate as to whether underemployment is more psychologically distressing than unemployment to individuals. While clearly underemployment is preferable to unemployment financially, there is some question as to whether prolonged underemployment leads to a sense of helplessness (Seligman, 1975) which is not readily reversible.

The length of time an individual is underemployed should be positively related to the level of his/her relative deprivation. The longer an individual is underemployed, the greater will be the distance between the individual's actual rewards and the ones he/she expects. Also, over a long period of underemployment, an individual is likely to see increasing numbers of colleagues in the same predicament receive more satisfactory employment themselves, heightening the contrast effect with comparative others. Furthermore, the longer the period of underemployment, the more likely the individual is to perceive the employment situation as irreversible (Feldman, 1996).

Along the same lines, the more active and energetic the job search, the greater the amount of relative deprivation experienced. Relative deprivation theory suggests that if individuals blame themselves for bad outcomes, they will experience less relative deprivation than if they blame external events (Crosby, 1976, 1984). Thus, if underemployed new graduates, laid-off workers, and contingent workers exert no effort to find new jobs, they may be unhappy with their employment situation but may not experience much relative deprivation since the remedy for their predicament is at least partially in their hands. Conversely, if underemployed workers expend considerable energy job hunting and still do not turn up satisfactory employment, their experience of relative deprivation is heightened. This suggests the next set of propositions regarding the degree of relative deprivation:

7A. The greater the time underemployed, the greater the relative deprivation.
7B. The more proactive and extensive the search for a satisfactory job, the greater the relative deprivation.

Mitigating/Exacerbating Circumstances

Previous research on procedural justice (Bies, 1987; Greenberg, 1987) and referent cognition theory (Folger & Martin, 1986) suggests that relative deprivation will be greater when individuals can easily envision alternative procedures for distributing rewards under which they would have fared better. In the context of underemployment, this suggests that underemployed workers will experience the most relative deprivation when the procedures which relegated the individuals into underemployment are seen as unfair and/or when the procedures which are used to promote or remove individuals from underemployment are seen as unfair.

Thus, in the case of underemployed laid-off workers, the degree of perceived unfairness of layoff procedures should be directly linked to the amount of relative deprivation. If laid-off workers view the procedures as "loaded" or unfairly designed to their disadvantage, then laid-off workers will attribute their predicament to external causes and have a heightened sense of relative deprivation (Brockner, 1990). Comparative others are getting a bettter deal, in short, and the organizations conducting the layoffs had it within their power to ensure a fairer set of outcomes.

In the case of involuntarily contingent workers, a major issue is whether the organizations are using "bait and switch" tactics to lure people into this type of employment (Feldman, Doespinghaus & Turnley, 1995). Many employment agencies which place temporary and part-time workers—and many organizations which hire contingent workers directly—implicitly or explicitly promise these workers that their jobs will convert to permanent status after some probationary period (usually 90–180 days). Many workers take contingent jobs as a way to obtain permanent employment, and when organizations renege on these perceived promises, contingent workers should experience greater amounts of relative deprivation because of the unfair tactics used to induce them to take these jobs.

Along the same lines, underemployed new college graduates should experience more relative deprivation when the selection procedures for jobs are perceived as unfair. In many cases, university placement procedures do not allow equal access of all graduates to all job postings. In addition, organizations' procedures for recruiting and selecting from the masses of applicants are sometimes haphazard and disorganized. When underemployed new graduates attribute their lack of success to unfair selection procedures, they experience a greater sense of relative deprivation, both because of the external attributions for their underemployment and because of the perceived unfairness related to comparison others (Feldman & Turnley, 1995).

This suggests the following propositions regarding the circumstances contributing to feelings of relative deprivation regarding underemployment:

8A. The greater the perceived unfairness of the layoff procedures, the more underemployed laid-off workers will experience relative deprivation.

8B. The greater the perceived unfairness of procedures for converting contingent employment into permanent employment, the more underemployed contingent workers will experience relative deprivation.

8C. The greater the perceived unfairness of selection procedures, the more underemployed new college graduates will experience relative deprivation.

The research on procedural justice (Greenberg, 1987) and moral outrage (Bies, 1987) suggests that when individuals receive bad outcomes they expect some type of organizational apology (or "penitential account") for the outcome and some signal that the organization is trying to make partial amends. In the context of underemployment, then, we would expect underemployed workers to experience less relative deprivation when the organization that caused or contributed to their becoming underemployed engages in behavior to ameliorate the negative effects of its actions.

Thus, the amount of assistance given to workers who end up underemployed due to layoffs should be inversely related to the amount of relative deprivation experienced. For instance, advance notification allows workers about to be laid-off a head-start on job hunting; severance pay and extended benefits help decrease the drop in income; providing outplacement and retraining opportunities decrease the chances laid-off workers will end up underemployed (Leana & Feldman, 1992, 1995). None of these organizational actions eliminate the underemployment directly, but they do signal both to laid-off workers and to survivors that the organization is trying to mitigate the immediate negative consequences of its actions.

In the case of underemployment contingent workers, we would expect those who receive pro-rated benefits based on hours worked per week to experience less relative deprivation than those who do not receive such benefits. One of the major issues facing many contingent workers is performing the same work duties as full-time, permanent employees, but receiving less job security, less pay, and fewer fringe benefits than their colleagues (Feldman, Doerpinghaus & Turnley, 1995). When organizations make some effort to provide at least some pro-rated benefits, underemployed contingent workers should experience less relative deprivation.

Similarly, the greater the amount of placement assistance given to graduating students, the less likely underemployed new graduates should experience relative deprivation. If students receive little or no assistance from school placement centers, they may attribute their underemployment to external forces (e.g., I had no access to job leads) and draw unfavorable comparisons to the fortunes of their friends at other schools who may be receiving considerably more assistance. On the other hand, if graduating students receive extensive assistance and still end up underemployed, they are more likely to make internal attributions for their failure and are less likely to experience relative deprivation.

Thus, the following propositions are offered:

9A. The greater the amount of assistance given to laid-off workers, the less likely underemployed laid-off workers will experience relative deprivation.

9B. Underemployed contingent workers who receive pro-rated benefits will feel less relative deprivation than those contingent workers who do not receive pro-rated benefits.

9C. The greater the amount of placement assistance given to graduating students, the less likely underemployed new graduates will experience relative deprivation.

CONCLUSIONS

We have proposed a variety of ways to utilize concepts from relative deprivation theory in future research on underemployment. In particular, we suggest that relative deprivation theory will be most instructive in understanding whom underemployed workers will choose as referent others, the degree of relative deprivation underemployed workers are likely to experience, and the circumstances that ameliorate/exacerbate the amount of relative deprivation experienced.

As theory development in this area moves into empirical testing, several issues should be considered. First, multiple measures of underemployment need to be utilized to capture both its objective components (e.g., loss of wages and job security) and its subjective components (e.g., perceived underutilization of skills and experience). Second, as much as possible, researchers need to let respondents identify *multiple* comparison others and specify whom they compare themselves with in assessing different facets of their job situations (Martin, 1981). Third, both underemployment and relative deprivation need to be conceptualized as continuous variables. There are degrees of underemployment and relative deprivation, and researcher-imposed dichtomous categorizations may miss many of the complexities of this phenomenon. Finally, in order to understand and untangle the effects of egoistic and fraternal deprivation, more intensive sampling of underemployed women, minorities and employees at different ages and career stages will be needed.

NOTE

Please address correspondence to Prof. Carrie R. Leana, Katz Graduate School of Business, University of Pittsburgh, 342 Mervis Hall, Pittsburgh, PA15260 USA. Tel. (412) 648-1674; Fax. (412) 648-1693; email Leana @ vms.cis.pitt.edu

REFERENCES

Ambrose, M. L. & Kulik, C. T. (1988) Referent sharing: Convergence within workgroups of perceptions of equity and reference choice. *Human Relations*, **41**, 697–707.
Bies, R. J. (1987) The predicament of injustice: The management of moral outrage. In L. L. Cummings & B. M. Staw (Eds.), *Research in Organizational Behavior*, Vol. 9, pp. 289–319. Greenwich, CT: JAI Press.
Borgen, W. A., Amundson, N. E. & Harder, H. G. (1988) The experience of underemployment. *Journal of Employment Counseling*, **25**, 149–159.
Brockner, J. (1990) Scope of justice in the workplace: How survivors react to co-worker layoffs. *Journal of Social Issues*, **46**, 95–106.
Burris, B. (1993) *No Room at the Top: Underemployment and Alienation in the Corporation*. New York: Praeger Press.
Cameron, K. S., Whetten, D. A. & Kim, M. U. (1987) Organizational dysfunctions of decline. *Academy of Management Journal*, **30**, 126–138.
Cropanzano, R. (Ed.) (1993) *Justice in the Workplace: Approaching Fairness in Human Resource Management*. Hillsdale, NJ: Erlbaum.
Crosby, F. A. (1976) A model of egoistical relative deprivation. *Psychological Review*, **83**, 85–113.
Crosby, F. A. (1982) *Relative Deprivation and Working Women*. New York: Oxford University Press.
Crosby, F. A. (1984) Relative deprivation in organizational settings. In B. M. Staw & L. L. Cummings (Eds.), *Research in Organizational Behavior*, Vol. 6, pp. 51–93. Greenwich, CT: JAI Press.
D'Aveni, R. A. (1989) The aftermath of organizational decline: A longitudinal study of the strategic and managerial characteristics of declining firms. *Academy of Management Journal*, **32**, 577–605.
Dornstein, M. (1989) The fairness of judgments of received pay and their determinants. *Journal of Occupational Psychology*, **62**, 287–299.
Dunn, L. F. (1979) Measuring the value of community. *Journal of Urban Economics*, **6**, 371–382.
Dyer, L. D. (1973) Job search success of middle-aged managers and engineers. *Industrial and Labor Relations Review*, **26**, 969–979.
Feldman, D. C. (1996) The nature and consequences of underemployment. *Journal of Management*, forthcoming.

Feldman, D. C., Doerpinghaus, H. I. & Turnley, W. H. (1995) Employee reactions to temporary jobs. *Journal of Managerial Issues*, **7**, 125–141.

Feldman, D. C. & Turnley, W. H. (1995) Underemployment among recent college graduates. *Journal of Organizational Behavior*, **16**, 691–706.

Folger, R. & Martin, C. (1986) Relative deprivation and referent cognitions: Distributive and procedural justice effects. *Journal of Experimental Social Psychology*, **22**, 531–546.

Goodman, P. S. (1974) An examination of referents used in the evaluation of pay. *Organizational Behavior and Human Performance*, **12**, 170–195.

Greenberg, J. (1987) Reactions to procedural injustice in payment distributions: Do the means justify the ends? *Journal of Applied Psychology*, **72**, 55–61.

Guimond, S. & Dubé-Simard, L. (1983) Relative deprivation theory and the Quebec Nationalist Movement: The cognition-emotion distinction and the personal-group deprivation issue. *Journal of Personality and Social Psychology*, **44**, 526–535.

Harrison, B. & Bluestone, B. (1988) *The Great U-turn: Corporate Restructuring and the Polarizing of America*. New York: Basic Books.

Henry, W. A. III. (1994) *In Defense of Elitism*. New York: Doubleday.

Jahoda, M. (1982) *Employment and Unemployment: A Social Psychological Analysis*. Cambridge: Cambridge University Press.

Kaufman, H. (1982) *Professionals in Search of Work*. New York: Wiley.

Kelly, H. H. (1973) The process of causal attribution. *American Psychologist*, **28**, 107–128.

Khan, L. J. & Morrow, P. C. (1991) Objective and subjective underemployment relationships to job satisfaction. *Journal of Business Research*, **22**, 211–218.

Langley, M. (1984) Many middle managers fight back as more firms trim their workforces. *Wall Street Journal* November 29, 55.

Leana, C. R. & Feldman, D. C. (1992) *Coping with job loss: How individuals, organizations, and communities respond to layoffs*. New York: Macmillan/Free Press.

Leana, C. R. & Feldman, D. C. (1995) Finding new jobs after a plant closing: Antecedents and outcomes of the occurrence and quality of reemployment. *Human Relations*, **48**, 1381–1401.

Marshall, G. (1984) On the sociology of women's unemployment, it neglect, and significance. *Sociological Review*, **32**, 234–259.

Martin, I. (1981) Relative deprivation: A theory of distributive injustice for an era of shrinking resources. In L. L. Cummings & B. M. Staw (Eds.), *Research in Organizational Behavior*, Vol. 3, pp. 53–107. Greenwich, CT: JAI Press.

Newman, K. S. (1988) *Falling from Grace*. New York: Free Press.

Newman, K. S. (1993) *Declining Fortunes: The Withering of the American Dream*. New York: Basic Books.

Novak, T. C. & Snyder, K. A. (1983) Woman's struggle to survive a plant shutdown. *Journal of Intergroup Relations*, **11**: 25–44.

O'Brien, G. E. & Feather, N. T. (1990) The relative effects of unemployment and quality of employment on the affect, work values, and personal control of adolescents. *Journal of Occupational Psychology*, **63**, 151–165.

Oldham, G. R., Kulik, C. T., Stepina, L. P. & Ambrose, M. L. (1986) Personal and structural correlates of the comparative referents used by employees. *Academy of Management Journal*, **29**, 599–608.

Quinn, R. P. & Mandilovitch, M. S. (1975) *Education and job satisfaction: A questionable payoff (NIE Papers in Education and Work, Vol. 5)*, Washington, D.C.: National Institute of Education.

Robinson, S. L., Kraatz, M. S. & Rousseau, D. M. (1994) Changing obligations and the psychological contract: A longitudinal study. *Academy of Management Journal*, **37**, 137–152.

Seligman, M. E. P. (1975) *Helplessness*. San Francisco: Freeman.

Stouffer, S. A., Suchman, E. A., DeVinney, L. C., Star, S. A. & Williams, R. M. (1949) *The American Soldier: Adjustment During Army Life*. Princeton, NJ: Princeton University Press.

Tilly, C. (1991) Reasons for the continuing growth of part-time employment. *Monthly Labor Review*, **114**, 10–18.

Turner, J. C., Oakes, P. J., Haslam, S. A. & McGarty, C. (1994) Self and collective: Cognition and social context. *Personality and Social Psychology Bulletin*, **20**: 454–463.

Winefield, A. H., Winefield, H. R., Tiggemann, M. & Goldney, R. D. (1991) A longitudinal study of the psychological effects of unemployment and unsatisfactory employment on young adults. *Journal of Applied Psychology*, **76**, 424–431.

CHAPTER 5

Effective Team Management and Cooperative Decisions in Chinese Organizations

Wang Zhong-Ming
Hangzhou University, CHINA

INTRODUCTION

Chinese management has its roots in ancient thinking and practices under the tradition of collective culture. Ideas of team management and group-oriented values were emphasized in the performance evaluation, personnel selection, quality control and project management. Popular Chinese values such as harmony relationship, being equal and average also reflected the color of the team concept. Team management has been considered as the Chinese approach to enhance collective traditions and spirit at work (Yang, 1984; Wang, 1993a; Bond, 1996). Values and culture are becoming the two key variables in studies of cross-cultural industrial and organizational psychology (Wang, 1992; Triandis, 1993; Wang & Satow, 1994; Smith & Wang, 1996).

Historically, Chinese management systems went through several models, from "three-men management" (1930s–1940s), "one-man management" (1950s), "director responsibility system under Communist Party leadership" (1960s) and "three-in-one revolutionary committee" (1970s) to the present "director responsibility system" in State-owned enterprises (1980–1990s). One significant historical experience has been that the collective and team approach is crucial to an effective management in China. The team structure of management (administrative director, party secretary and union representative) originated from the revolutionary areas in 1930s and 1940s has been the dominating system while the Soviet-type of one-man management in

Trends in Organizational Behavior, Volume 4. Edited by C. L. Cooper and D. M. Rousseau.
© 1997 John Wiley & Sons Ltd.

1950s was ineffective partly due to its inconsistency with the Chinese collective leadership models (Wang, 1995).

The recent economic reform and management change since 1978 have facilitated a shift from egalitarianism to task responsibility. Because of the delay in the managerial and structural change, this shift, to a large extent, strengthened the individualist management practice, weakened the traditional collectivist systems but provided new opportunities for the development of more effective team management in China. In particular, with the rapid development of international joint ventures in China, cross-cultural coordination and adaptation have become an important aspect of management. Team building and management has become a major topic for management training and executive development. As a result of the recent organizational reform in Chinese enterprises, topic such as team incentives, group responsibility systems, group adaptation, team conflict resolution, group compatibility and cooperative decision making have become the focus of Chinese organizational behaviour. The new trend in organizational behaviour has been facilitated by the management reform and organizational change in Chinese enterprises. In this chapter, I will start with the group management practices following the Chinese economic development and then review some recent organizational behaviour research so as to build up a more comprehensive model of Chinese team management.

CHINESE ORGANIZATIONAL CONTEXT FOR TEAM WORK

There are several Chinese cultural traditions that have important effects on the team management practice and the development of organizational behaviour in China. The group has been reinforced since 1949, including areas of group decision making, team work, group reward and group cohesiveness. During the recent economic reform, group approach has been more encouraged as one of the Chinese characteristics of management practice with the new emphasis of team responsibility. Also, harmony relationships among team members have been again emphasized. Good relationships across and/or within organizational levels are considered crucial to a successful management. Although more responsibility and competition among companies has been encouraged in recent years, many people who were used to egalitarianism could not easily adapt to the new situations of inter- and within-organizational competitions. In most organizations, linking individual interests with the group and organizational interests has been greatly encouraged to facilitate higher organizational commitment and effectiveness. These cultural traditions of group approach are affecting organizational behaviour or Chinese enterprise and other organizations during the recent decade of economic reform.

Team approach has been especially effective in quality management which is characterized as "expert mass joint quality control". In relation to this approach, interpersonal relationship in teams is emphasized as crucial to a successful management. Chinese employees have a close attachment to their work units for most of organizations provide housing, medical care, children's day-care, and services for retired employees. China has a long tradition of group approach in management but has suffered from the "iron rice bowl" (i.e., guaranteed employment and guaranteed pay irrespective of performance) during the 1950s through 1970s, which led to low work efficiency. In the early 1980s, as a reaction to the "iron rice bowl" problem in pay distribution, an individualistic approach to piece-rate bonus system emphasizing individual performance became popular in some of Chinese industries (Wang, 1990; Wang, 1995).

Current Chinese team management context has been largely influenced by the two major nationwide movements: the "excellent group evaluation campaign" in the 1960s and the "optimization through regrouping" in 1980s and early 1990s. The first managerial movement emphasized group cohesiveness and modelling behavior. As an effective approach to labor emulation, titles such as "excellent team" and "excellent enterprise" have been used as a kind of social reward for work groups or enterprise organizations with good morale and performance. Each year, there are public campaigns at national, provincial, city or enterprise levels for evaluating and awarding these excellent team or enterprise titles. It is also an important approach to improve and facilitate both team and organizational developments. However, during the 1950s and early 1960s, this excellent team movement focused mostly upon team technical innovations and cooperations. Some examples of excellent work groups were the Ma Hengchang Group with excellent group technical management, the Liu Changfu Group with good group accounting management and the Zhao Mengtao Group with sound group cooperation, all of which were nominated by their group leaders. Research indicated that a high degree of group involvement and a good fit between task requirements and group goals with clear member responsibility are the keys to team excellence and team goal-directed behaviour (Wang, 1993a). Many excellent work teams were developed through the autonomous management of quality circle (QC) in the nationwide quality control activities. There is a national QC evaluation campaign for the excellent quality circle award every year. The excellent team/enterprise movement has greatly enhanced group and organizational commitment, cohesiveness and performance in Chinese industries and other organizations. This managerial movement was successful in the 1960s and strengthened by the Chinese participation model at Ansan Steel Company, the "two-way participation, one reform and three-in-one combination" (Xu, J.Z., 1984). This influential management principle was developed from a popular nationwide management practice in 1960s. "Two-way participation" represents the participation of workers in top management and cadres (managers and supervisors) in daily shopfloor operations. "One reform" is to change unreasonable management regulations and improve management systems. "Three-in-one combination" is to encourage cadres, technicians, and workers to work closely in technical innovations and management. This nationwide practice was successful in enhancing management efficiency and morale, stressing the importance of mass mobilization, participation, and Communist Party leadership in management and production.

The second managerial movement focused upon team–job fit and group task responsibility. Although team approach was widely adopted during the 1950s and 1960s in Chinese enterprises, work groups were exclusively organized and appointed by the management. This produced problems such as over-staffing and low responsibility. With the deepening of economic reform, team efficiency became a bottleneck for most enterprises. Since the late 1980s and early 1990s, the "optimization through re-grouping" has been implemented among more than 6000 state-owned enterprises. Supervisors of work groups were asked to re-organize their teams on the basis of voluntary grouping and skills. This initiative has achieved positive results. The two nationwide movements of team management have created a favorable organizational context emphasizing both group cohesiveness and team responsibility.

Since team efficiency has become a key to organizational effectiveness, some experimental programs of team development were then carried out to improve group autonomy and efficiency. Among them, a field experiment was conducted to find out the effects of voluntary groupings of work team on group cohesiveness and productivity, using sociometric methods and involving 136 workers in a number of factories (Wang, 1993a). A unique characteristic of this experiment was that a voluntary grouping was conducted under close supervision of the managers who could make some adjustment of the experimental groupings according to employees' ability, skill, and attitudes. Comparisons were made between 14 experimental groups (voluntary groupings) and 14 control groups (assigned by the management). The results of this field experiment showed that the experimental group as a whole had significantly higher daily output and more positive attitudes toward work and the company than that of the control group.

With the development of Chinese economic reform, it was more and more evident that the traditional way of assigning group membership by the management was not effective in enhancing team cooperation and performance. This reform practice has been implemented in coordination with the introduction of the labor contract system, seen as a solution to the problem of the "iron rice bowl". The new system emphasizes work responsibility and allows enterprises and workers to choose each other, which has been a big development towards decentralization and high efficiency in management in China. Yu (1988) studied the effects of such labor contact systems in three groups in a company in Shanghai. It was found that comparing to the conventional system, the new voluntarily based team system improved interpersonal relationships and social climate within groups, enhanced formal leadership and participation in team management and led to higher performance. One of the Chinese characteristics of group management is that the formal group system has been more group behaviour whereas the informal group is relatively weak and often in good coordination with the formal one. A psychological survey conducted as a television factory revealed that group norms for performance were mainly based upon the formal production quota system rather than the informal ones (Xu, X.D., 1986).

EFFECTS OF GROUP INCENTIVE SYSTEM ON PERFORMANCE

The recent Chinese economic reform started with a nationwide initiative in motivating employees through changes in work and incentive systems, and it emphasized task responsibility. This led to a more individualistic approach to incentive design such as a piece-rate bonus system. This practice discouraged collective responsibility and weakened team effectiveness. Surveys in early 1980s showed that a more flexible and comprehensive multiple reward structure (combining social rewards with material incentives) should be used in order to motivate the Chinese work force (Wang, 1986, 1988). In a field experiment using a flexible multi-reward system in a steel file company in Beijing, workers who completed their production targets could choose an incentive from five alternatives: cash bonuses, technical training, leaving early for home, group vacation and the excellent-worker title. The experimental group resulted in significant higher motivation and doubled productivity (Chen, 1989).

In addition, some studies were carried out to examine the effects of group incentive systems on performance. In a field experiment, an individual responsibility system was compared with the group responsibility systems, under either success or failure work situations, using chain assembly tasks and attribution measurements of five factors (effort, ability, cooperation, task and chance). The results showed that workers' attributions of success and failure had significant impact upon their subsequent behavior and performance. This effect was greatly affected by the organizational and structural characteristics of incentive systems. Under the group system, workers tended to attribute their performance to team cooperation and collective efforts which may maintain or enhance their motivation and expectancy for future performance; whereas under the individual system, workers more frequently attributed their performance to some personal factors or task difficulty which reduced their motivation. An implication of this study was that a team-oriented incentive system with group responsibility structure would be more effective in facilitating morale, cooperation and productivity in Chinese organizations. Under the team responsibility system, the work team as a whole was responsible for the production task and the incentive was mainly based on team performance.

In another quasi-experiment, Wang (1988, 1994) implemented a five-week team attributional training program in which each work team met in a workshop once a week after work to discuss their performance. Objective attributions about their success and failure were encouraged. The results showed that the team attributional training did reduce workers' attributional biases, enhance their work motivation and result in better mutual understanding, cooperation and performance.

FACTORS IN TEAM CONFLICT MANAGEMENT

Another aspect of team management is how groups deal with inconsistency and conflicts within the groups. Since China has a tradition of favoring harmony and relationship, conflict was considered as a problem in teams. However, under the recent organizational reform and re-grouping, conflict is seen as a drive for team development. Wang and Wu (1996) completed a large scale research on team conflict and team climate and their effects on performance. Altogether, 314 employees from 61 teams in 40 organizations were studied. Among them, 37 teams were from the Chinese State-owned companies, 12 teams from joint ventures and another 12 teams from private companies. Nearly one third were from manufacturing industry and two thirds from service industry. The results showed special dynamics in the Chinese team management.

- *Individual-level factors in team management.* At individual level, there are significant differences between Chinese State-owned companies and international joint ventures in such factors as group interaction, conflict resolution, value orientation and group belongings. Specifically, employees in State-owned companies expressed a significantly higher degree of group interaction (especially informal interaction), better conflict resolution, stronger group belonging and higher level of cooperative value orientation.

- *Group-level factors in team management.* At group level, there was only significant difference between Chinese State-owned companies and international joint-ventures in conflict resolution, i.e., a more positive conflict management in the State-owned systems. While State-owned companies showed no difference from that of the privately owned companies, this difference could be attributed to the cross-cultural and international business settings.

- *Effects of team management.* There were significant effects of team management upon team climate, including group communication, innovations, objectives perception, participation and task accomplishment. The higher the group interaction, the stronger the team tendency towards cooperation, the better the quality of conflict management.

- *Structural and organizational influence.* The effects of team management on team climate were influenced by the management structures in the organizations such as State-owned, joint ventures and private systems. Under the State-owned system, both group interaction and value orientation had more general positive effects upon team climate while conflict resolution mainly affected communication and group belonging. Under the joint venture system, both group interaction and value orientation had less effect on team climate but conflict resolution played an important role in determining the team climate. However, under the private owned system, group interaction had no effects on team climate while both value orientation and conflict resolution played positive roles.

Under the present economic reforms, while Chinese management is moving towards more decentralized and market-oriented, and internationalist stage, there has been a trend from collectivism to individualistic working style (Wang & Heller, 1993). Therefore, team management has become more important and significant. Both research and application of Chinese organizational behavior focused upon team effectiveness in the early 1980s when the major task in the economic reform was to reorganize and adjust the work force to the new approach in management and production.

Chinese society very much emphasized collectivism, social interaction and team approaches in work situations. Especially since 1949, team building has been very popular in enterprise management. Even after the "cultural revolution" when individual responsibility was encouraged, belonging to groups was still considered as a priority in the needs structure of Chinese employees. However, in the recent nationwide management reform, this cultural tradition has been given new meaning but emphasizing group responsibility and team effectiveness (Wang, 1986, 1988). Team approach has become a major strategy in the Chinese economic reform program. This approach has integrated group responsibility, authority with team interests and enhanced work motivation and efficiency. In another field study on conflict management among 41 teams, Wang and Zhu (1996) investigated the relationships between team conflict management approaches and performance. The following managerial and structural implications were put forward.

- *Effects of ownership and organizational structures.* Compared with teams in State-owned companies, teams from international joint ventures tended to adopt a problem-solving approach, use conflict avoidance and less cooperative strategies, and be more serious in evaluation of subordinates' performance. In the service industry, teams in joint ventures adopted more competitive strategies than non-joint ventures but, in manufacturing industry, teams from non-joint ventures used more competitive strategies than joint ventures.
- *Relationship between team management and performance.* Team commitment and mutual support had no direct effects on team efficiency but acting upon performance through an intervening variable, i.e., high involvement. However, the conflict avoidance strategy may facilitate members' mutual support and commitment but affect members' task involvement and in turn reduce team efficiency.
- *Strategies in conflict management.* Conflict strategies had important influences on members' subsequent behavior. A competitive strategy reduced members' mutual support and team commitment whereas a cooperative strategy with opening discussion enhanced their cooperation and self-management.

These recent research have provided systematic evidence about the processes of team conflict management in Chinese organizations. Ownership and organizational/structural factors have played crucial roles in shaping the team behavior.

GROUP COMPATIBILITY IN COOPERATIVE DECISIONS

Team behavior is not only affected by the organizational and structural contingencies, but also shaped by the characteristics of team members. Among other things, team compatibility is a significant characteristic.

Team members with high team compatibility tend to share information and psychological resources and exchange ideas with other members. Strasser and Titus (1985) and Strasser (1992) studies the process of information sharing and used a method of hidden profiles to examine the importance of information sharing in group decision making. In recent years, with the development of economic reform and organizational change, team compatibility has become a more important factor in team management. Wang and Lu (1996) completed a series of experiments in defining and analyzing team compatibility. Three components of team compatibility are identified: active cooperation, communicative coordination, and information sharing.

- *Active cooperation.* Active cooperation is characterized as group value orientation, group interests and group resources management style. Through active cooperation, team members work closely toward team objectives.
- *Communicative coordination.* Communicative coordination emphasizes team communication and joint working effort. Under communicative coordination, team members are provided with specific directions and plans.
- *Information sharing.* Information sharing focuses upon comprehensive and multi-directional information exchange. It emphasizes key task information and integrated team objectives.
  In order to measure team compatibility, both the dilemma game and the nuts game were used. Two major strategies were demonstrated: "win-stay, lose-change" and "win-cooperate, lose-defect". In the groups of high team compatibility, members tended to adopt a strategy of "win-stay, lose-change" but less used the "win-cooperate, lose-defect". However, in the groups of low compatibility, members more used "win-cooperate, lose-defect" strategy while less adopting a "win-stay, lose-change" strategy. There were significant differences between these two groups in using the "win-stay, lose change" strategy but not in the use of "win-cooperate, lose-defect" strategy. In addition, members in the higher team compatibility groups used more strategies of problem solving and concession whereas members in the lower team compatibility groups members tend to adopt more competitive strategies.

CONCLUSIONS: TEAM MANAGEMENT & STRATEGIC HRM

Team management and cooperative decision making process have been important topics of human resources management and organizational behavior in China. With the rapid development of Chinese market economy and international joint ventures in recent years, team management has been greatly emphasized. In many international joint ventures as well as large State-owned enterprises, team building has been seen as an effective approach to strategic human resource management. As a new trend of organizational behavior in China, team and cooperative work is becoming an active area in theoretical studies and practical applications.

ACKNOWLEDGEMENT

This study was supported by a research grant from the Chinese National Science Foundation to WANG Zhong-Ming.

REFERENCES

Chen, L. (1989) Organization development in China: Chinese version. *Chinese Journal of Applied Psychology*, **4:** 1–5.

Bond, M.H. (1996) *The Handbook of Chinese Psychology*. Hong Kong: Oxford University Press.

Smith, P.B., Wang, Z.M. (1996) Chinese leadership and organizational structures. Chapter 2 In M. Bond (Ed.) *Handbook of Chinese Psychology*, (Chapter 21, pp. 322–337). Oxford: Oxford University Press.

Strasser, G (1992) Information salience and the discovery of hidden profiles by decision-making groups: A "thought experiment". *Organizational Behaviour and Human Decision Processes*, **52:** 156–181.

Strasser, G. & Titus, W. (1985) Pooling of unshared information in group decision-making: biased information sampling during group discussion. *Journal of Personality and Social Psychology*, **48:** 1476–1478.

Triandis, H.C. (1993) Cross-cultural industrial and organizational psychology. In M.D. Dunnette & L.M. Hough (Eds.) *Handbook of Industrial and Organizational Psychology* (2nd edn), Vol. 4, Chapter 43. Palo Alto, CA: Consulting Psychologists Press.

Wang, Z.M. (1986) Worker's attribution and its effects on performance under different work responsibility systems. *Chinese Journal of Applied Psychology*, **1:** 6–10.

Wang, Z.M. (1988) The effects of responsibility system change and group attributional training on performance: A quasi experiment in a Chinese factory. *Chinese Journal of Applied Psychology*, Vol. 3, No. 3: 7–14.

Wang, Z.-M. (1990) Action research and organization development strategies in Chinese enterprises. *Organizational Development Journal*, Spring, 66–70.

Wang, Z.-M. (1992) Managerial psychological strategies for Sino-foreign joint-ventures, *Journal of Managerial Psychology*, **7:** 10–16.

Wang, Z.-M., Heller, F.A. (1993) Patterns of power distribution in organizational decision making in Chinese and British enterprises, *International Journal of Human Resource Management*, **4(1),** 113–128.

Wang, Z.-M. (1993a) Culture, economic reform and the role of industrial/organizational psychology in China. In M.D. Dunnette & L.M. Hough (Eds), *Handbook of Industrial and Organizational Psychology* (2nd edn), pp. 689–726. Palo Alto, CA: Consulting Psychologists Press.

Wang, Z.-M. (1993b) Psychology in China: A review dedicated to Li Chen. *Annual Review of Psychology*, **44**: 87–116, Palo Alto, CA: Annual Review.

Wang, Z.-M. (1994) Group attributional training as an effective approach to human resource development under team work system. *Ergonomics*, **37** (7) 1137–1144.

Wang, Z.-M. (1995) Chinese management. In M. Warner (ed.), *International Encyclopaedia of Business and Management*, London: Routledge.

Wang, Z.-M. & Lu, X.H. (1996) A process model of group decision making and the structural analysis of team compatibility. The working report for the project supported by the Chinese National Science Foundation.

Wang, Z.-M. & Satow, T. (1994) The effects of structural and organizational factors on socio-psychological orientation in joint ventures. *Journal of Managerial Psychology*, Special Issue: Managing Chinese-Japanese Joint Ventures, **9** (4) 22–30.

Wang, Z.-M. & Wu, T.X. (1996). The effects of team management on team climate and work efficiency. The working report for the project supported by the Chinese National Science Foundation.

Wang, Z.-M. & Zhu, L.Z. (1996). Team conflict management and its relationship with performance under different industries and organizational systems. The working report for the project supported by the Chinese National Science Foundation.

Xu, J.Z. (1984) Two way participation, one reform and three-in-one combination. In *Chinese Encyclopaedia of Enterprise Management* (Chinese), pp. 90, Beijing: Enterprise Management Press.

Xu, X.D. (1986) Effects of production quota increase on workers' performance. *Information on Psychological Sciences* (in Chinese), No. 6, 36–42.

Yang, D.N. (1984) Management thought in ancient China. In *Chinese Encyclopaedia of Enterprise Management* (in Chinese), pp. 245. Beijing: Enterprise Management Press.

Yu, W.Z. (1988) The motivational function of group structure under labor contract systems. *Behaviour Science* (in Chinese), No. 1, 80.

CHAPTER 6

Letting Them Down Gently: Conceptual Advances in Explaining Controversial Organizational Policies

D. Ramona Bobocel
University of Waterloo

and

Richard L. McCline and Robert Folger
Tulane University

INTRODUCTION

Imagine you are a manager of a company in which a decision has just been made to adopt an affirmative action policy. Knowing that the policy is controversial, how do you minimize potential negative reactions by employees? On the basis of a body of research in the area of organizational justice, some might recommend that you offer employees an explanation for the policy. What would this entail precisely?[1]

Recent research on organizational justice has demonstrated that, under certain conditions, managerial explanations can enhance employees' perceptions of fairness of organizational decisions that portend negative outcomes (for reviews, see Bies, 1987; Folger & Bies, 1989; Konovsky & Brockner, 1993; Konovsky & Cropanzano, 1993; Greenberg, 1993b; Tyler & Bies, 1990). It is often recommended, therefore, that managers should

---

[1]Although some of the present work was stimulated by questions we had regarding the communication of affirmative action policies, the ideas we delineate here do not necessarily apply only to that context.

Trends in Organizational Behavior, Volume 4. Edited by C. L. Cooper and D. M. Rousseau.
© 1997 John Wiley & Sons Ltd.

offer explanations for organizational decisions in an effort to minimize the potential for negative reactions.

Several concepts appear to be particularly central in the literature on managerial explanations. For instance, research conducted by Bies and Shapiro and their colleagues has shown that, to be effective, explanations must be perceived as adequate and sincerely delivered (e.g., Bies & Shapiro, 1987, 1988; Bies, Shapiro & Cummings, 1988; Shapiro, 1991; Shapiro, Buttner & Barry, 1994; Sitkin & Bies, 1993). Research conducted by Greenberg (1990, 1993a, 1993b, 1994) has shown that explanations are effective when they provide thorough, or detailed, information about the reasons for a policy and when they are delivered with interpersonal sensitivity.

Although past research has informed us well about certain issues, in some of our recent research (e.g., Bobocel & Farrell, 1996; Folger, McCline & McDannell, 1994) we found that there were important questions that the present literature could not fully address. For example, precisely what does it mean to give an adequate explanation for a controversial organizational policy, such as affirmative action? How do the issues of thoroughness of information, sincerity, and sensitivity relate to the concept of adequacy? Despite its central role in the literature on explanations, there is little published research (a notable exception is the recent work of Shapiro and her colleagues; Shapiro, 1991; Shapiro, Buttner & Barry, 1994) that has systematically examined what constitutes an adequate explanation.

Before future research can begin to address systematically some of the questions issued above, we will need to do more conceptual work to guide our predictions and to help interpret results. Accordingly, the primary goal of the present paper is to set out one broad conceptual framework that might be useful in directing future research on the managerial communication of controversial organizational policies.

Managerial explanations can be considered as a form of persuasive communication (e.g., Heath, 1994; Nutt, 1990). Thus, we believe it is possible to integrate some of the existing findings, as well as to offer directions for future empirical work, by drawing on a distinction made in the social psychological literature on persuasion, as well as in the broader psychological literature on social judgment, between systematic and heuristic processing. Depending on employees' processing strategy, this could have implications for (a) which variables influence their perceptions of the adequacy of an explanation and attitudes toward the policy being explained, (b) how such reactions are mediated, and (c) the persistence of their attitudes toward the policy.

In the next sections of the paper, we first provide a general overview of the systematic-heuristic processing distinction and relevant research. Second, we discuss how the distinction might apply to the context of managerial explanations. Third, we outline major conceptual and research implications. Although we recognize that it is not the only framework that can be used to advance conceptual and empirical work on managerial explanations, we believe it is one that might prove quite useful.

SYSTEMATIC AND HEURISTIC PROCESSING

It has long been recognized in the psychological literature on social judgment that, sometimes, perceivers carefully process available information and make decisions based on the evidence at hand (e.g., Anderson's, 1971, information integration theory). At other times, however, perceivers rely on simple rules, or cognitive heuristics, that allow them to make judgments without much thought or effort (e.g., Kahneman & Tversky, 1973; Nisbett & Ross, 1980; Sherman & Corty, 1984). These two styles of processing actually represent endpoints of a continuum of possible approaches to making social judgments, ranging from mindful to mindless (Langer, 1978) or from controlled to automatic (Schneider & Shiffrin, 1977).

Given that attitudes are a form of social judgment, it is not surprising that attitude theorists have made a similar distinction in the persuasion literature. Specifically, attitude theorists have distinguished between systematic and heuristic processing—two cognitive processing strategies that people may employ when deciding whether to accept or reject the overall position contained in a persuasive communication (for a review, see Chaiken, 1987; cf. Petty & Cacioppo, 1981, 1986, for a similar but not identical distinction between the central and peripheral routes to persuasion).

In brief, systematic attitude change is said to result from considerable cognitive effort that individuals expend attending to, elaborating, rehearsing, and integrating the arguments contained in a persuasive communication. In contrast, heuristic attitude change is said to result from the application of simple decision rules or schemes that are presumably learned from past experiences and observations (e.g., "I should agree with experts"; "the greater number of arguments, the stronger the message"; "if the majority agrees, it must be right"). Compared with systematic processing, persuasion via heuristic processing is said to occur with much less cognitive effort on the part of recipients. As the examples above illustrate, it is argued that heuristic processing can involve decision rules that refer to communicator cues (e.g., expertise), message cues (e.g., number of arguments), or cues in the persuasion context (e.g., audience response).

Perceivers tend to process the content of a message more carefully and rely less on simple decision cues under certain conditions. For example, numerous studies have shown that systematic processing is more likely when the issue is highly (rather than less) involving (Eagly & Chaiken, 1984; also see Liberman & Chaiken, 1996, and Petty & Cacioppo's, 1986, elaboration–likelihood model) and when individuals have greater (rather than less) ability to engage in issue-relevant thought (e.g., Wood, Kallgren & Priesler, 1985).

In addition to motivation and ability to process, other variables have been found to moderate processing strategy. For example, several studies have shown that the salience or vividness of extrinsic cues increases reliance on heuristic processing (e.g., Pallak, 1983). Moreover, individual difference variables (need for cognition, uncertainty orientation) have been shown to relate to processing strategy (e.g., Cacioppo, Petty & Morris, 1983; Sorrentino et al., 1988).

Systematic and heuristic processing are conceptualized as parallel modes, and, therefore, they may be utilized simultaneously. Nevertheless, in situations where the recipient is highly motivated and has the ability to engage in processing of the message content, systematic processing is postulated to reduce the effect of extrinsic cues (unless they are particularly salient or vivid) that might otherwise have been processed heuristically (Chaiken, 1987; Petty & Cacioppo, 1986).

We draw on the general systematic-heuristic processing distinction as a framework that might help to integrate the role of several concepts that are prominent in the literature on managerial explanations, as well as to potentially reconcile inconsistencies in research findings. Furthermore, this analysis provides a stimulus and guide for future research. The core elements of the processing distinction, as they might pertain to the context of managerial explanations of organizational policies, are presented schematically in Figure 6.1. Note that although managerial explanations can affect several dependent variables—such as employees' perceptions of the message sender (e.g., Bies, Shapiro & Cummings, 1988), as well as the organization (e.g., Greenberg, 1994)—we focus in the present paper on understanding employees' perceptions of the adequacy of a managerial explanation and attitudes toward the policy being explained.

In the next section, we elaborate on the elements in Figure 6.1; in a subsequent section, we highlight some specific areas for future research.

EXPLAINING CONTROVERSIAL ORGANIZATIONAL POLICIES

Explanation Event

Consistent with the view of several justice theorists (e.g., Bies, Shapiro & Cummings, 1988; Greenberg, 1990, 1993a, 1993b, 1994; Shapiro, 1991;

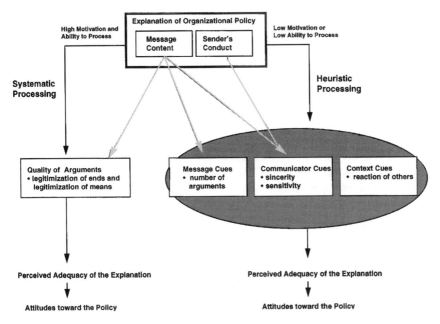

Figure 6.1 Possible determinants of employees' perceptions of the adequacy of explanations of organizational policies and attitudes toward the policy being explained, as a function of their systematic or heuristic processing strategy

Shapiro, Buttner & Barry, 1994) and as shown in Figure 6.1, a managerial explanation can be thought of as comprising two general elements: the content of the message (e.g., what the manager says) and the interpersonal conduct of the message sender (e.g., the demeanour of manager). Note that, in a sense, various features of a message's content (e.g., its extensiveness) can themselves be conceptualized as one aspect of conduct—namely, indicating an act of choice on the message giver's part to use this particular content rather than some other. Thus, it is likely that the two elements are somewhat naturally related (e.g., see Shapiro, Buttner & Barry, 1994, Studies 1 & 2).

Determinants of Processing Strategy

Depending on situational or intrapersonal variables, employees should process the explanation either heuristically or systematically (or through some combination of both strategies). An individual who is heuristically processing should presumably evaluate the explanation chiefly through the application of simple decision rules, rather than through issue-relevant thinking. (Note that what we mean by the term heuristic processing differs from what others refer to as a fairness heuristic—see Lind et al., 1993, and Messick, 1993).

As shown in Figure 6.1, we conceptualize the notions of sincerity (i.e., truthfulness or openness; Baron, 1988; Bies & Moag, 1986; Tyler & Bies, 1990) and interpersonal sensitivity (i.e., concern for recipients over outcomes received; Greenberg, 1990, 1993a, 1993b, 1994) as communicator cues that can be processed heuristically. This is because an employee might agree with a manager who is sensitive or sincere, not because he or she thought deeply about what the manager said, but rather because the manager appears to be trustworthy (Meyerson, Weick & Kramer, 1996). Other heuristic cues might pertain to the message (e.g., "How long is the explanation?"), or to the organizational context (e.g., "How do coworkers respond?").

Thus, employees who are processing an explanation heuristically might rely largely on extrinsic cues to form their judgments of the explanation's adequacy, and, in turn, their attitudes toward the policy being explained. Attitudes toward the policy, arrived at this way, might tend to be relatively unstable (e.g., Chaiken, 1980).

In contrast to those processing heuristically, employees who are motivated and have the ability to process systematically should carefully scrutinize the content of the managerial explanation. Reactions should be determined largely by the strength, or quality, of the arguments and the nature (e.g., favorable or unfavorable) of recipients' issue-relevant thoughts, elicited by the message. Attitudes formed this way should be relatively enduring. We discuss possible determinants of message strength in a subsequent section.

Perceptions of the Adequacy of an Explanation

As discussed earlier, at present it is not clear conceptually what recipients mean when they rate an explanation as adequate. Do ratings of adequacy necessarily reflect the strength, or quality, of the message arguments? We believe the answer is no. In other words, we separate the issue of the strength, or quality, of the message arguments from the issue of explanation adequacy.

As noted by Shapiro and her colleagues (Shapiro, Buttner & Barry, 1994, Study 1), it is possible that ratings of an explanation's adequacy reflect recipients' acceptance of, or satisfaction with, that explanation. If this were so, then, as they argue, an explanation could be rated as adequate for a variety of reasons, some of which might not relate to argument quality at all. More specifically, we suggest that an individual who is processing heuristically (rather than systematically) might judge an explanation as adequate (i.e., satisfactory or acceptable) largely on the basis of surface-level content, communicator, or context cues. Argument quality should affect judgments of adequacy only for those who are systematically processing the explanation.

By considering processing strategy, this analysis makes it clearer conceptually why adequacy ratings can be but are not necessarily an indication of the strength, or quality, of the message content. Put differently, it helps to specify, a priori, which classes of variables might influence perceptions of adequacy (and attitudes toward the policy) and under what conditions they should be stronger or weaker determinants.

FUTURE RESEARCH DIRECTIONS

The preceding analysis has several implications for future research on managerial explanations of controversial organizational policies. In this section, we outline some possible research directions.

Moderators of Processing Strategy

One strategy for future research on managerial explanations would be to investigate directly both situational and intrapersonal variables that might moderate employees' processing strategy.

A situational variable that traditionally has played an important role in the broader justice literature (for a review, see Brockner & Wiesenfeld, 1996) and that might be particularly relevant here is outcome negativity, or outcome severity. For instance, Greenberg (1994) found that employees were more accepting of a corporate smoking ban when the company president offered an explanation that was high (rather than low) in information thoroughness and also when it was offered in a socially sensitive versus insensitive manner—moreover, these effects were stronger for heavy smokers, individuals for whom the outcome was self-rated as most negative, as compared with nonsmokers or light smokers (also see Greenberg, 1990, 1993a, 1993b). Thus, in Greenberg's study, the explanation components had a stronger beneficial effect on employee acceptance when the event being explained was particularly negative.

More recently, Shapiro and her colleagues showed that outcome negativity might have a more complex moderating effect on perceptions of explanation adequacy. In an initial correlational study, they found that the beneficial effect of explanations (which were self-reported by recipients as logical in content and delivered by a concerned manager) were stronger when the outcome being explained (failure to receive a job offer) was rated as *less* versus more negative. In a follow-up vignette study, the researchers manipulated the specificity of the content of an explanation, the sincerity of delivery, and the severity of the outcome being explained (a poor grade that ostensibly either would or would not interfere with students' ability to graduate). The researchers found that adequacy was determined by *different* explanations features, depending on outcome severity. In conditions of low severity, specificity of content and sincerity of delivery had an additive relation; whereas, in conditions of high severity, the two elements had a multiplicative relation.

Drawing on the systematic-heuristic processing framework, it might be possible to reconcile such inconsistencies in findings pertaining to outcome severity. That is, as outcome severity increases, motivation to process might increase, but, at some point, ability to process could begin to decrease (i.e., at very high levels of severity, affect might be so high as to prevent systematic processing; Easterbrook, 1959; Yerkes & Dodson, 1908; also see Nemeth, 1986). If this were true, then systematic processing might be more likely to occur at moderate levels of outcome severity, and, at either of the extreme ends heuristic processing might prevail. Therefore, depending on the level of outcome severity in a particular study, different components of an explanation might be more or less influential determinants of perceptions of adequacy, and, in turn, attitudes.

Other research on moderators could examine the role of the salience or vividness of extrinsic cues or of individual differences in processing style. This line of research would enable us to better understand the conditions under which different variables (e.g., quality of content vs. communicator characteristics) have more or less influence on perceptions of the adequacy of an explanation and attitudes toward the policy being explained. To this end, the research could help to integrate the literature on managerial explanations.

Heuristic Processing

As shown in Figure 6.1, the present analysis suggests a number of elements that might be influential under conditions of heuristic processing. For example, researchers could investigate directly the role that message content cues such as the mere number of arguments have on employees' reactions, under conditions of low versus high-involvement.

Similarly, the role of contextual features, such as the extent to which others agree or disagree with the message, could be examined (also see Folger et al., 1979). Most of the early research on managerial explanations (e.g., Bies & Moag, 1986; Bies, Shapiro & Cummings, 1988) examined individuals' reactions to explanations of decisions that affected them specifically (e.g., no job offer, denial of a special request). More recently, however, researchers have begun to study the role of explanations for policies that affect many people, such as layoffs (see Konovsky & Brockner, 1993), a wage freeze (Greenberg, 1990), a smoking ban (Greenberg, 1994), and employee drug-testing (Konovsky & Cropanzano, 1993). In contrast to explaining decisions that affect only an individual, the potential for context effects becomes more obvious in the case of explaining controversial organizational policies.

In the next sections, we specify some directions for future research on the concepts of communicator sincerity and sensitivity, given their prominence in the current literature.

Sincerity

As shown in Figure 6.1, it is possible to construe the issue of communicator sincerity, or truthfulness, in two ways that are not necessarily mutually exclusive. That is, as one would intuitively predict, sincerity might be communicated and inferred from the conduct of the message giver—by his or her nonverbal manner or tone of speech, for example. Alternatively, sincerity might not be conveyed by the sender's conduct *per se*, but instead by aspects of the content of the message itself (Shapiro, Buttner & Barry, 1994). In other words, sincerity might be viewed as a property of the content of a message, which, in turn, influences one's attribution of the sender.

We suggest that future research should attend to both these possibilities. Research on heuristically processed judgments could help establish which surface-level characteristics, both of the content of an explanation and of the message-giver, convey sincerity. Only by discovering which aspects of a message itself might convey sincerity— specific expressions, or tone and style—can we learn whether ratings about the sincerity of a message giver are due to that person's perceived qualities (e.g., perhaps based on heuristically processed cues about demeanour), due to some qualities of the message content, or both.

Sensitivity

As with sincerity, sensitivity might be conveyed either by some aspect of the message-sender's conduct, the message content, or both. Thus, the message content might be processed heuristically for evidence of sensitivity, and a conclusion that the message displays sensitivity might tend to imply that it had been transmitted by a sensitive person—that is, someone who shows concern and respect for the dignity of recipients.

The connection we are suggesting between the message content and either the sensitivity or the sincerity attributed to the communicator raises a theoretical point with respect to announcements about any type of corporate policy. Specifically it suggests that a detailed, information-laden message (e.g., Greenberg, 1994) might have a substantial effect on attitudes for either of two reasons, or because of some combination of both. On the one hand, a detailed message might be influential because of systematic processing and issue-relevant thinking. On the other hand, a detailed message might be processed heuristically as conveying sincerity or sensitivity on the part of the communicator.

There is a practical implication to this point, as well. It would mean that communicators who expect people to react heuristically to an issue (perhaps because it is very emotional) could go astray if they thereby confined their efforts exclusively to delivering messages that contained only surface-level cues, without attention to the quality of the arguments. That is, even when people are heuristically processing and, therefore, not engaging in issue-relevant thinking, a high quality message (with a reasonably substantial quantity of detail) could prompt conclusions about the communicator's sincerity and sensitivity.

Systematic Processing

Quality of Arguments

Given that individuals who are systematically processing should scrutinize the content of the explanation, what contributes to a cogent message? As noted earlier, several justice researchers have examined elements of the content of explanations that contribute to their effectiveness. For example, Shapiro and her colleagues found that the specificity of feedback for a negative decision (operationalized as the extent to which it was personalized, or particular to the individual) enhanced individual's ratings of adequacy. Greenberg (1990, 1993b, 1994) showed the beneficial effect of giving employees a high amount of information about the reasons for adopting a policy.

As shown in Figure 6.1, we extend this line of research on message content by drawing on the existing distributive–procedural dichotomy in the broader justice literature to distinguish between explanations aimed at "legitimizing the ends" and those aimed at "legitimizing the means."

By legitimizing the ends, we mean that the explanation focuses on providing the reasons why a particular end goal (or outcome)—to be achieved through the organizational policy—is desirable and, therefore, should be valued by employees. For example, one might legitimize the ends by appealing to desirable superordinate goals or values, a tactic similar to what has classically been called a justification (e.g. Schlenker, 1980; Scott & Lyman, 1968) or an ideological account (Bies, 1987).

We should note that it is possible for a message sender to legitimize the ends not only by describing the desirable, or positive, goals that could be gained (as illustrated above), but also by describing negative goals that could be avoided (for other work on framing of goals, see Levin et al., 1995; Dutton & Duncan, 1987; Roney, Higgins & Shah, 1995; Smith & Petty, 1996).

Although it is possible to legitimize the ends by stating both the positives that might be gained and the negatives that might be avoided, the two methods are not entirely similar—the latter could imply that the sender was forced by mitigating circumstances to behave in some manner. In this way, legitimizing the ends in terms of stating the negatives that might be avoided could resemble what has classically been called an excuse (e.g., Schlenker, 1980; Scott & Lyman, 1968) or a causal account (Bies, 1987). We avoid using the traditional distinction between excuses and justifications, because, as illustrated above, depending on whether it is framed in positive or negative terms, an explanation aimed at legitimizing the ends sometimes can be considered to be either an excuse or a justification.

In contrast to legitimizing the ends, by legitimizing the means, we refer to an explanation where the content focuses on giving information about procedural issues: This might include information about the procedures by which a policy came to be developed, as well as the manner in which it will be implemented in the organization.

In sum, paralleling the general distributive–procedural justice distinction, the content of an explanation can be conceptualized as focusing on legitimizing the ends (a distributive focus) versus the legitimizing the means (a procedural focus). Moreover, just as sometimes it is useful to further distinguish procedural justice into (a) the specific processes leading to a decision, and (b) the manner in which those processes are enacted (i.e., interactional justice, see Bies & Moag, 1986), an explanation that legitimizes the means might similarly include either or both information about the actual procedures by which a policy came to be (e.g., "Did all relevant parties have voice?"; "Was accurate information used?"), and the manner in which it will be implemented in the organization (e.g., "Will employees be told about decisions with timeliness and courtesy, by someone using candor and honesty in stating why the decision was made?").

Future research is necessary to examine the independent and/or interaction effects of explanations that legitimize the ends and those that legitimize the means (under conditions of systematic versus heuristic processing) on employees' judgments. For example, it is possible that, when employees are systematically processing, an explanation that merely legitimizes the ends might be insufficient—although it could be necessary—to affect ratings of adequacy, and, in turn, attitudes toward the policy. In other words, because they are systematically processing, employees might not only look for information in an explanation that legitimizes why a policy is being implemented (i.e., the ends), but also they might expect information that legitimizes the procedures (i.e., the means).

Certain inconsistencies in results between existing studies on managerial explanations might reflect differences in the way researchers have operationalized explanation content. For example, in the experiment reported by Shapiro, Buttner & Barry (1994, Study 3 noted earlier), it appears that the manipulation of explanation specificity was operationalized similar to our definition of legitimizing the means. As they state, "Subjects in the *high specificity condition* received specific and personalized informational regarding how the final grade was computed, including a brief discussion of how their individual attendance, class participation, and final exam score led to the failing grade. Subjects in the *low specificity condition* received information which said only that department rules do not permit a passing grade given their performance" (pp. 361–362).

In contrast, in Greenberg's (1994) smoking ban study discussed earlier, the manipulation of information thoroughness involved giving employees either a high amount of detail or a low amount of detail regarding the reasons for adopting the smoking ban, an operationalization that corresponds to our definition of legitimizing the ends. It also appears that in Greenberg's study, the ends were legitimized chiefly by pointing to negatives (e.g., company costs, health problems) that might be avoided, rather than to positives that could be gained.

Apart from other potential differences across these studies, the difference in the manner in which the explanation content appears to have been operationalized (as legitimizing the means versus the ends, respectively) might have contributed to the inconsistency in findings noted earlier.

Process Research

Another avenue for future research on managerial explanations suggested by systematic–heuristic analysis is research to test the process that mediates employees reactions.

In brief, the goal of research on process would be to test directly one's assumptions about whether systematic or heuristic processing (or some combination of both) was indeed mediating observed effects. This line of research would involve examining the nature of recipients' cognitive responses (for an excellent review of common methodologies, see Perloff, 1993).

Only by understanding what goes through employees' minds when they receive (or anticipate) an explanation will we fully understand how managerial explanations operate on attitudes. Thus, we believe it would be useful for future research to focus directly on understanding the underlying cognitive process, in addition to showing attitudinal effects.

CONCLUSIONS

In conclusion, drawing on theory and research in other areas of psychology, we suggested that employees' perceptions of the adequacy of managerial explanations of controversial organizational policies, as well as their attitudes toward the policies being explained, might be influenced by different variables depending on how the communication is cognitively processed.

The present framework has important conceptual implications, and, although it is only one possible way of thinking, it might help to integrate several concepts that are prominent in the existing literature on managerial explanations. Moreover, it offers a useful guide for future research. For example, future research could examine variables that moderate the determinants of employees' reactions, as well as investigate further the surface-level cues that might be heuristically processed. In addition, we think that (rather than focusing exclusively on the traditional distinction between excuses and justifications) research might benefit from exploring the implications of legitimizing the ends, or goals, of a policy in various ways and of legitimizing the means whereby those policy goals were decided on, as well as the means of implementing them.

Finally, we have alluded only briefly to the practical implications of the processing strategy analysis, but we think they are of obvious importance. Controversial organizational policies such as diversity or affirmative action programs can elicit strong emotional reactions. The proposed framework applies work on the cognitive–emotional interface of message processing to illustrate that the impact of managerial communication practices in such domains can draw on rich sources of available concepts.

ACKNOWLEDGEMENTS

This article was drafted while the first author was a Visiting Professor at the Centre for Administrative Studies at the University of Western Ontario. We gratefully acknowledge Liane Davey, John Meyer, John Michela, Denise Rousseau, and Leanne Son Hing for their valuable comments on earlier drafts of this article.

NOTE

Please address correspondence to Dr. Ramona Bobocel, Department of Psychology, University of Waterloo, Waterloo, Ontario, Canada N2L 3C1. Tel: (519) 888-4567 (ext. 3622); fax (519) 746-8631; email rbobocel@watarts.uwaterloo.ca. Dr. Richard McCline is now at San Francisco State University.

REFERENCES

Anderson, N.H. (1971) Integration theory and attitude change. *Psychological Review*, **78**, 171–206.

Baron, R. (1988) Attributions and organizational conflict: The mediating role of apparent sincerity. *Organizational Behavior and Human Decision Processes*, **41**, 111–127.

Bies, R.J. (1987) The predicament of injustice: The management of moral outrage. *Research in organizational behavior*, **9**, 289–319.

Bies, R.J. & Moag, J.S. (1986) Interactional justice: Communication criteria of fairness In R.J. Lewicki, B.H. Sheppard & M.H. Bazerman (Eds.) *Research on negotiations in organizations* (Vol. 1, pp 43–55). Greenwich, CT: JAI Press.

Bies, R.J. & Shapiro, D.L. (1987) Interactional fairness judgments: The influence of causal accounts. *Social Justice Research*, **1**, 199–218.

Bies, R.J. & Shapiro, D.L. (1988) Voice and justification: Their influence on procedural fairness judgments. *Academy of Management Journal*, **31**, 676–685.

Bies, R.J. Shapiro, D.L. & Cummings, L.L. (1988) Causal accounts and managing organizational conflict: Is it enough to say it's not my fault? *Communication Research*, **15**, 381–399.

Bobocel, D.R. & Farrell, A. (1996) Sex-based promotion decisions and interactional fairness: Investigating the influence of managerial accounts. *Journal of Applied Psychology*, **81**, 22–35.

Brockner, J. & Wiesenfeld, B.M. (1996) The interactive impact of procedural fairness and outcome favorability: The effects of what you do depend on how you do it. *Psychological Bulletin*, **2**, 189–208.

Cacioppo, J.T. Petty, R.E. & Morris, K.J. (1983) Effects of need for cognition on message evaluation, recall, and persuasion. *Journal of Personality and Social Psychology*, **45**, 805–818.

Chaiken, S. (1980) Heuristic versus systematic information processing and the use of source versus message cues in persuasion. *Journal of Personality and Social Psychology*, **39**, 752–766.

Chaiken, S. (1987) The heuristic model of persuasion. In M.P. Zanna, J.M. Olson & C.P. Herman (Eds.), *Social influence: The Ontario Symposium*, Vol. 5, pp. 3–39).

Hillsdale, NJ: Lawrence Erlbaum.

Dutton, J.E. & Duncan, R.B. (1987) The creation of momentum for change through the process of strategic issue diagnosis. *Strategic Management Journal*, **8**, 279–295.

Eagly, A.H. & Chaiken, S. (1984) Cognitive theories of persuasion. In L. Berkowitz (Ed.), *Advances in Experimental Social Psychology*, Vol. 17, pp. 268–359. Hillsdale, NJ: Lawrence Erlbaum.

Easterbrook, J.A. (1959) The effect of emotion on the utilization and the organization of behaviour. *Psychological Review*, **66**, 183–201.

Folger, R. & Bies, R.J. (1989) Managerial responsibilities and procedural justice. *Employee Responsibilities and Rights Journal*, **2**, 79–90.

Folger, R., McCline, R.L. & McDannell, J. (1994) What makes you think this policy is fair? Paper presented at the National Academy of Management, Dallas, Texas, USA.

Folger, R., Rosenfield, D., Grove, J. & Corkran, L. (1979) Effects of "voice" and improvement on experienced inequity. *Journal of Personality and Social Psychology*, **37**, 2253–2261.

Greenberg, J. (1990) Employee theft as a reaction to underpayment inequity: The hidden cost of pay cuts. *Journal of Applied Psychology*, **75**, 561–568.

Greenberg, J. (1993a) Stealing in the name of justice: Informational and interpersonal moderators of theft reactions to underpayment inequity. *Organizational Behavior and Human Decision Processes*, **54**, 81–103.

Greenberg, J. (1993b) The social side of fairness: Interpersonal and informational classes of organizational justice. In R. Cropanzano (Ed.), *Justice in the workplace: Approaching fairness in human resource management*, pp. 79–103. Hillsdale, NJ: Lawrence Erlbaum.

Greenberg, J. (1994) Using socially fair treatment to promote acceptance of a work site smoking ban. *Journal of Applied Psychology*, **79**, 288–301.

Heath, R.L. (1994) Management of corporate communication: From interpersonal contacts to external affairs. Hillsdale, NJ: Lawrence Erlbaum.

Kahneman, D. & Tversky, A. (1973) On the psychology of prediction. *Psychological Review*, **80**, 237–251.

Konovsky, M.A. & Brockner, J. (1993) Managing victim and survivor layoff reactions: A procedural justice perspective. In R. Cropanzano (Ed.), *Justice in the Workplace: Approaching Fairness in Human Resource Management*, pp. 79–103. Hillsdale, NJ: Lawrence Erlbaum.

Konovsky, M.A. & Cropanzano, R. (1993) Justice considerations in employee drug testing. In R. Cropanzano (Ed.), *Justice in the workplace: Approaching Fairness in Human Resource Management*, pp. 79–103. Hillsdale, NJ: Lawrence Erlbaum.

Langer, E.J. (1978) Rethinking the role of thought in social interaction. In J.H. Harvey, W.J. Ickes & R.F. Kidd (Eds.), *New Directions in Attribution Research*, Vol. 2, pp. 35–58. Hillsdale, NJ: Lawrence Erlbaum.

Levin, I.P., Schneider, S.L., Gaeth, G.J. & Conlon, A.B. (1995) All frames are not created equals: A typology of valence framing effects. Unpublished manuscript.

Liberman, A. & Chaiken, S. (1996) The direct effect of personal relevance on attitudes. *Personality and Social Psychology Bulletin*, **22**, 296–279.

Lind, E.A., Kulik, C.T., Ambrose, M. & de Vera Park, M.V. (1993) Individual and corporate dispute resolution: Using procedural fairness as a decision heuristic. *Administrative Science Quarterly*, **38**, 224–251.

Messick, D.M. (1993) Equality as a decision heuristic. In B.A. Mellers & J. Baron (Eds.), *Psychological Perspectives on Justice: Theory and Applications* (pp. 11–31). New York: Cambridge University Press.

Meyerson, D., Weick, K.E. & Kramer, R.M. (1996) Swift trust and temporary groups. In. R.M. Kramer & T.R. Tyler (Eds.), *Trust in Organizations: Frontiers of Theory and Research*. Thousand Oaks, CA: Sage.

Nemeth, C. (1986). The differential contribution of majority and minority influence. *Psychological Review*, **93**, 1–10.

Nisbett, R.E. & Ross, L. (1980). *Human Inference: Strategies and Shortcomings of Social Judgment*. Englewood Cliffs, NJ: Prentice-Hall.

Nutt, P.C. (1990) Preventing decision debacles. *Technological Forecasting and Social Change*, **38**, 159–174.

Pallack, S.R. (1983) Salience of a communicator's physical attractiveness and persuasion: A heuristic versus systematic processing interpretation. *Social Cognition*, **2**, 156–168.

Perloff, R.M. (1993) *The Dynamics of Persuasion*. Hillsdale, NJ: Lawrence Erlbaum.

Petty, R.E. & Cacioppo, J.T. (1981) *Attitudes and Persuasion: Classic and Contemporary Approaches*. Dubuque, IA: W.C. Brown.

Petty, R.E. & Cacioppo, J.T. (1986) The elaboration likelihood model of persuasion. In. L. Berkowitz (Ed.), *Advances in Experimental Social Psychology*, Vol. 19, pp. 123–205. New York: Academic Press.

Roney, C.J.R., Higgins, E.T., Shah, J. (1995) Goals and framing: How outcome focus influences motivation and emotion. *Personality and Social Psychology Bulletin*, **21**, 1151–1160.

Schlenker, B.R. (1980). *Impression Management: The Self-Concept, Social Identity, and Interpersonal Relations*. Monterey, CA: Brooks-Cole.

Schneider, W. & Shiffrin, R.M. (1977) Controlled and automatic information processing: I. Detection, search, and attention. *Psychological Review*, **84**, 1–66.

Scott, M.B. & Lyman, S.M. (1968) Accounts. *American Sociological Review*, **33**, 46–62.

Shapiro, D.L. (1991) The effects of explanations on negative reactions to deceit. *Administrative Science Quarterly*, **36**, 614–630.

Shapiro, D.L., Buttner, E.H. & Barry, B. (1994) Explanations: What factors enhance their perceived adequacy? *Organizational Behavior and Human Decision Processes*, **58**, 346–368.

Sherman, S.J. & Corty, E. (1984) Cognitive heuristics. In R.S. Wyer & T.K. Srull (Eds.), *Handbook of Social Cognition*, Vol. 1, pp. 189–286. Hillsdale, NJ: Erlbaum.

Sitkin, S.B. & Bies, R.J. (1993) Social accounts in conflict situations: Using explanations to manage conflict. *Human Relations*, **46**, 349–370.

Smith, S.M. & Petty, R.E. (1996) Message framing and persuasion: A message processing analysis. *Personality and Social Psychology Bulletin*, **22**, 257–268.

Sorrentino, R.M., Bobocel, D.R., Gitta, M.Z., Olson, J.M. & Hewitt, E.C. (1988) Uncertainty orientation and persuasion: Individual differences in the effects of personal relevance on social judgments. *Journal of Personality and Social Psychology*, **55**, 357–371.

Tyler, T.R. & Bies, R.J. (1990) Beyond formal procedures: The interpersonal context of procedural justice. In J. Carroll (Ed.), *Advances in Applied Social Psychology: Business Settings* pp. 77–98. Hillsdale, NJ: Lawrence Erlbaum.

Wood, W., Kallgren, C.A. & Priesler, R.M. (1985) Access to attitude-relevant information in memory as a determinant of persuasion: The role of message attributes. *Journal of Experimental Social Psychology*, **21**, 73–85.

Yerkes, R.M. & Dodson, J.D. (1908) The relation of strength of stimulus to rapidity of habit formation. *Journal of Comparative Neurology of Psychology*, **18**, 459–482.

CHAPTER 7

The Continuing "American Dilemma": Studying Racism in Organizations

Arthur P. Brief and Erika L. Hayes

A. B. Freeman School of Business and Department of Psychology, Tulane University

- "Over the past few years, the government and news media have shown more respect to Blacks than they deserve."
- "Discrimination against Blacks is no longer a problem ... "
- "Blacks are getting too demanding in their push for equal rights."

Endorsement of the above statements is an indication of racism (McConahay, Hardee & Batts, 1981). In this chapter, we will explain why this is so, at least in the United States, and will demonstrate the implications of our explanation for the study of race relations in contemporary work organizations. We suspect that for many, if not most readers, the statements are *not* consistent with what they construe of as representative racist beliefs. Indeed, the kind of racism we will be writing about is not the sort we think is often evoked by use of the label "racist". The set of beliefs attached to this label frequently is associated with the kind of racism described by Gunnar Mydral in his 1944 classic on race relations, *An American Dilemma*. What Mydral saw, more than five decades ago, was a White America that generally embraced a blatant kind of racism, now termed "old-fashioned." Alternatively, this chapter focuses on a new kind of racism, one not yet clearly evident in the organizational science literature.

Our principal contention in this chapter will be that significant advances in understanding workplace race relations is dependent upon

Trends in Organizational Behavior, Volume 4. Edited by C. L. Cooper and D. M. Rousseau.
© 1997 John Wiley & Sons Ltd.

appreciating the nature of racial attitudes surrounding contemporary organizations and incorporating that appreciation into our research agendas. Two reasons for presenting this argument will be offered. First, workplace race relations are an enduring problem. Second, organizational scientists have not adequately fulfilled their responsibility for informing discussions of how this problem might be resolved.

The remainder of the chapter unfolds as follows. We begin with a highly selective review of the evidence showing that Black Americans remain targets of discrimination in employment. Next, we very briefly discuss how organizational scientists have an obligation to help alleviate such victimization. Then, the tenets of both old-fashioned and the new kind of racism in the United States are presented. The latter portions of this presentation will emphasize the likely role of seemingly harmless "business justifications" in releasing the beast of the new kind of racism. To demonstrate the utility of considering the new kind of racism, examples of recent investigations of workplace race relations are provided in which explicit examination of the construct would have been informative. That is, even though the new kind of racism has yet to be measured in an organizational field study, research results from organizations are evident that can be usefully interpreted in terms of the construct. Following this demonstration, a number of pressing research questions are posed whose answers have implications for understanding the organizational experience of Black Americans as well as other victims of employment discrimination.

THE PROBLEM AND THE OBLIGATION

It is only logical to establish racial discrimination as a workplace problem prior to addressing responsibilities for alleviating it. This section, therefore, opens with a brief argument that Black Americans are often the victims of discrimination in the employment arena. For broader and more detailed discussion of racial discrimination in the United States see, for example, Blauner (1989), Essed (1991), and van Dijk (1987).

According to the United States Census Bureau, the real income of White families, between 1979 and 1993, increased by 9%, but the income of Black families did not budge. More germane to our current purpose, the Census Bureau also reported that Blacks, in 1993, earned less than their White counterparts in all jobs, at all levels. In addition, Blacks very rarely make it up organizational hierarchies to the ranks of senior management; they comprise only 0.2 to 0.3% of those at that level (Braham, 1987).

The above descriptive statistics could be a product of several factors. For instance, Blacks might earn less than their White counterparts and more move up as far because of relatively lower levels of human capital (e.g., job relevant knowledge, skills, and abilities). In fact, research shows, for example, meaningful differences in some abilities (e.g., Jensen, 1985) that, at least in part, are attributable to the lower socioeconomic status of Blacks in the United States (e.g., White, 1982). What follows, however, demonstrates that the differential outcomes experienced by Blacks also can be explained by racial discrimination.

During the 1992–1993 fiscal year, more than 52 000 allegations of racial discrimination were filed with the United States Equal Employment Opportunity Commission against private sector employers. These allegations, of course, do not constitute proof but some of the settlements of such charges do indicate the problem is real and severe. For example, in late 1992, Shoney's agreed to pay $132.5 million in response to allegations that the restaurant company discriminated against its Black employees. Only 1.8% of Shoney's restaurant managers were Black; and, 75% of its Black restaurant employees held jobs in three low-paying, non-customer contact positions (e.g., dishwasher) (Watkins, 1993). Consistent with this sort of case evidence are the findings of an interesting study by Bendick, Jackson & Reinoso (1994). In the greater Washington, D.C. area, they sent teams comprising a Black and a White matched in terms of sex, age, personal appearance, articulateness, and manner out to apply for the same jobs. The pairs also were equipped with similar fictional job qualifications. While Blacks were favored over Whites in 5% of the encounters with prospective employers, Whites are favored over Blacks in 29% of them. Indeed, Black applicants often were told a job already was filled while their White counterparts were granted interviews for the "filled" openings.

Another interesting study shows that racial discrimination continues beyond the hiring process. In a study of clerical employees in a large Northeastern commercial bank, Blacks were found to be four times more likely than Whites to be assigned, after five months on the job, to a Black supervisor (Lefkowitz, 1994). When the researcher who discovered this pattern of segregation queried the bank's management about it, he received an enlightening response. Not only did they claim they were unaware of the pattern; the managers professed no knowledge of any policy or custom of job assignments that would lead to segregation of employees by race. While top management may proclaim to be unaware of employee segregation, such patterns do not necessarily go undetected at lower levels. Based on interviews from middle level managers in a financial services company, Hayes (1995) discovered that this group may in fact be painfully aware of employee segregation. Implying that ethnic and cultural similarity to top management was important to one's future career success, one middle level manager stated "Ethnic background is important because things are localized here. For example, there is the Jewish department, or West European department, the "old boy" department, or the professional female division".

The above examples are consistent with a recent review of the organizational literature that indicates "unobtrusive studies show a clear picture of racism" (Stone, Stone and Dipboye, 1992, p. 411). In part, we took the time to make this point because, as will be seen, a characteristic of those harboring new kinds of racist attitudes is their belief that racial discrimination is a thing of the past. Given that we are confronting an enduring problem, who is obliged to help alleviate it? One obvious answer is that the promotion of a just society, one that embraces the value of equality, is the responsibility of all its members (e.g., Rawls, 1971). We think organizational scientists, because of their unique ability to produce knowledge relevant to alleviating the problem, have a particularly heavy obligation. That is, expertise in understanding the thoughts, feeling, and actions of people at work is not burden free; we have a responsibility to apply this expertise in ways that serve to enhance the quality of people's organizational lives (e.g., Nord, 1977). Thus, the question becomes, have we met our obligations to the victims of racial discrimination and, thereby, to promoting a more just society through applying our expertise?

While we have cited some exceptions and the number of them appear to be increasing, we concur with Cox and Nkomo (1990) that a read of the organizational literature would lead one to believe that organizations are race neutral. In other words our research does not adequately reflect the problem of racial discrimination. (Also see Nkomo (1992)). Thus, we have failed to meet our collective obligation. Our values have been reflected in the research questions we have chosen to pursue (Kaplan, 1964); and, therefore, we have elected, perhaps unknowingly, to maintain the status quo (e.g., Baritz, 1960). Below, we leave behind explicit considerations of the obligations, values, and societal role of the organizational scientist and attempt to entice the reader to action by demonstrating how intellectually interesting the study of racism in organizations can be and by suggesting how such research might generally inform our understandings of attitudes, social cognitions, interpersonal relations, group processes, and individual differences in organizations, both within the United States and beyond. We begin with a discussion of the new kinds of racism.

A NEW KIND OF RACISM

Mydral (1944) described the United States as a country whose majority population openly endorsed White supremacy and, correspondingly, Black inferiority as well as public policies promoting racial segregation in virtually all aspects of people's lives. For example, derogatory statements about Blacks' innate intelligence were commonplace and separation of the races in education, housing, and access to public facilities the norm. As we will show, all of this is largely a thing of the past; and, the beliefs of White Americans during that period safely can be labelled as "old-fashioned" racism (e.g., Sniderman & Tetlock, 1986).

Likely in part because the Holocaust gave racism a horrific name, old-fashioned racial attitudes among Whites began to change after World War II; and, since the passage of the United States Civil Rights Act of 1964, the results of various public opinion polls make it clear that attitudes towards Blacks among White Americans have become more tolerant (e.g., Greeley & Sheatsley, 1971; Smith & Sheatsley, 1984; Taylor, Sheatsley, & Greeley, 1978). Given that old-fashioned racism can be considered dying if not dead in the United States, why then do so many Whites continue to resist attempts to bring about real racial equality? A group of psychologists, principally interested in the racial aspects of political attitudes and behaviours, have addressed this question. They were concerned with understanding, for example, White opposition to busing and affirmative action as means of achieving racial integration as well as to Black candidates running for public office. These psychologists have considered two explanations for such opposition (cf. Kinder, 1986).

First, Whites resist racial change because of their perception that Blacks pose a real threat in their lives (e.g., to their personal safety, their children's education, and their jobs). Data indicate, however, that White opposition to racial busing, antagonism towards affirmative action programs, and votes against Black candidates are *independent* of the racial threats they see themselves facing in their personal lives (e.g., Kinder & Rhodebeck, 1982; Kinder & Sears, 1981; Sears, Hensler & Speer, 1979).

Second, White resistance to racial change is a product of the blending of a residue of negative racial sentiments and such treasured American values as individualism and self-reliance (Kinder, 1986). Numerous studies, in fact; show that old-fashioned racism has been transmuted to more subtle, indirect, and rationalizable types of racial bigotry (e.g. Crosby, Bromley & Saxe, 1980; Katz, 1981; Kinder & Sears, 1981; McConahay, 1983; Sears & Allen, 1984) reflective of this blend. These new kinds of racism tolerate Whites, for instance, endorsing the principle of equal opportunity and, at the same time, vociferously opposing affirmative action. While conceptual distinctions can be seen among these new kinds of racism (e.g. Kinder, 1986; Sears, 1988, Dovidio & Gaertner, 1991; Sniderman et al., 1991), their common essence is captured in the works of McConahay and his associates (e.g., McConahay, 1983; McConahay, Hardee & Batts, 1981).

According to McConahay (1986, pp. 92–93),

> "the principal tenets of modern racism are these: (1) Discrimination is a thing of the past because Blacks now have the freedom to complete in the marketplace and to enjoy those things they can afford. (2) Blacks are pushing too hard, too fast, and into places where they are not wanted. (3) These tactics and demands are unfair. (4) Therefore, recent gains are undeserved and the prestige granting institutions of society are giving Blacks more attention and the concomitant status than they deserve."

In addition, McConahay describes two other tenets of modern racism: (a) the first four tenets do not constitute racism because they are empirical facts; and (b) racism is bad. Consequently, "those endorsing the ideology of modern racism do not define their own beliefs and attitudes as racist" (McConahay, 1986, p. 93) and they act in ways to protect a nonprejudiced, nondiscriminatory self-image. Thus, for the modern racist to behave consistently with his/her negative racial attitudes requires that he/she be imbedded in "a context in which there is a plausible, nonprejudiced explanation available for what might be considered prejudiced behavior ..." (McConahay, 1986, p. 100).

Let us recap McConahay's (1986) depiction of modern racism, for it is so central to our story. Modern racists *think* racism is socially undesirable yet *feel* negatively towards Blacks partially because they believe the gains Blacks have made were not earned. Even though their negative feelings predispose modern racists to say and do things harmful to Blacks, their desire not to be seen by themselves or others as prejudiced hold these tendencies in check. Modern racists are released to speak or act out against Blacks *only* when they have an excuse which protects them from the charge of racism. For example, a modern racist is freed to oppose busing to achieve racial integration by the justification that school buses are unsafe. Without such plausible, nonprejudiced explanations, modern racists will behave no differently towards Blacks than their non-bigoted White counterparts.

In most research, consistent with extant theorizing, the plausible, nonprejudiced explanations used to free modern racists to act on their negative attitudes have been designed to enhance the saliency and potency of *non-racial* factors that would justify unfavorable responding regardless of the race of the target person. (See, for example, Gaertner (1976) and Gaertner and Dovidio (1981).) As we explore the implications of modern racism for understanding race relations in organizations, we begin with a consideration of justifications that are explicitly *racial* in nature. Reizenstein and Brief (1995), following the lead of Brief et al. (1995), have empirically demonstrated that these race-based justifications, so long as they appear to be nonprejudicially motivated, also release modern racists to act on their negative attitudes. Later, we detail Reizenstein and Brief's study.

Recall the case of Shoney's. A former Vice-President stated the restaurant company's discriminatory practices were the result of the Chief Executive Officer's (CEO) unwritten policy that "Blacks should not be employed in any position where they would be seen by customers" (Watkins, 1993, p. 424). The CEO himself admitted "In looking for anything to identify why is this unit under-performing, in some cases, I would probably have said this is a neighborhood of predominantly White neighbors, and we have a considerable amount of Black employees and this might be a problem" (Watkins, 1993, p. 427). At lower levels of the organization, such analyses by the CEO translated into some managers feeling they needed to "lighten-up" their restaurants—a company euphemism for reducing the number of Black employees—and to hire "attractive White girls" instead (Watkins, 1993).

As you can see, Shoney's CEO reasoned that a restaurant's performance is affected positively if the racial make-up of the unit's customer contact personnel *matched* the customer population served. Thus, a unit serving a White customer population should employ, according to the reasoning of the CEO, White customer contact personnel. We believe that the reasoning of Shoney's CEO, reflecting a bottom-line business perspective, may be seen as plausible and may appear to many managers as nonprejudicial. Moreover, we believe such reasonings are commonplace in business organizations *and*, as asserted above, serve to release the beast of modern racism.

The ideas of a "business justification to discriminate", at first glance, may seem far-fetched. It is not. Prior to the civil rights movement, these justifications were explicitly part of the content of management education. Take, for instance, the lesson taught by Chester I. Barnard in his classic 1938 *The Functions of the Executive*. He described the informal executive organization whose purpose is to communicate "intangible facts, opinions, suggestions, suspicions, that cannot pass through formal channels" (p. 225). In order for this informal organization to operate effectively, Barnard prescribed selecting and promoting people to executive positions that *match* those already in place. He stated "Perhaps often and certainly occasionally men cannot be promoted or selected, or even must be relieved, because they cannot function, because they 'do not fit' where there is no question of formal competence. This question of 'fitness' involves such matters as education, experience, age, sex, personal distinctions, prestige, race ... " (p. 224). More than three decades after the publication of Barnard's advice to executives, a Black manager wrote "I believe that many of the problems I encountered were of fit ... I was out of 'place' normally filled by Black people in the company ... " (Jones, 1973, p. 114).

Today, "race matching rules" have not disappeared from the management education literature. Using the same business logic as Shoney's CEO, however, these rules are advanced by those advocating racial integration (e.g., Cox, 1993). The President of Avon Corporation, for example, concluded that his company's inner-city markets became significantly more profitable when additional Black and Hispanic contact personnel customer were placed in them (Cox & Blake, 1991). This was so, according to the President, because newly placed personnel were uniquely qualified to understand certain aspects of the world view of the minority populations in the inner city.

We contend it is naive to believe that if an organization uses a matching rule to include Blacks, the use of the same sort of rule to exclude Blacks is precluded. While the staffing consequences of the two forms of the rule are different, they both rest on the same business logic—racial matching enhances organizational effectiveness.

As we have shown, justifications to discriminate occur when one advocates racially matching customers and employees (as was done by Shoney's CEO) and when one advocates person–organization fit in terms of race (as was done by Barnard). The later matching rule warrants further discussion, for we are particularly fearful of its prevalence in practice. This fear stems from the increasing attention person–organization fit ideas are getting in the practice literature (e.g., Bowen, Ledford & Nathan, 1991) and from research findings indicating that organizations do select people like those already in place (e.g. Schneider, 1987). Obviously, fit is not often explicitly discussed in regards to race; rather, it is addressed in terms of attitudes, beliefs, personality, style, and/or values, often vaguely defined. This vagueness too easily could allow the modern racist to unknowingly translate a concern for person–organization fit into a concern for race, one that constitutes a plausible, non-prejudicially motivated business justification to discriminate. Assume, for example, a modern racist decides to exclude from consideration a Black job candidate for a position in an all White workgroup. His decision reflected a concern for potentially disrupting interpersonal relations in a group whose members work well together. He also did not want to unfairly burden the Black job candidate with the costs of adjusting in a workgroup whose members might provide less than a warm reception. The modern racist simply sees his decision as an appropriate managerial response to these realistic concerns. Indeed, he might even see his decision not "to unfairly burden" the Black job candidate as an expression of his nonracist attitudes.

In sum, we have argued that racial discrimination in the employment arena can be explained, in part, by a more "subtle, indirect, and rationalizable" form of bigotry than old-fashioned racism. This new form, modern racism, only explains discriminatory behavior, however, when a plausible, nonprejudiced justification for the behavior is available. This justification is required because modern racists do not want to be seen by themselves or others as bigots. Indeed, their racial attitudes can be said to be unconscious (Banaji & Greenwald, 1994). It is the unconscious nature of modern racism that leads it to be described as "subtle, indirect, and rationizable." Moreover, we asserted that the justifications necessary to release modern racists to act on their negative attitudes can be race based as well as racially free in content. Finally, we argue that, in the workplace, they may be quite common and be termed "business justification to discriminate".

Does modern racism, in fact, operate in organizations in a fashion consistent with our arguments? A study by Reizenstein and Brief (1995) speaks to this question. The researchers administered a measure of modern racism (McConahay, Hardee & Batts, 1981) prior to subjects' participating in a laboratory experiment. In the experiment, the subjects, acting in the belief that they were assisting a professor with a consulting project, reviewed the credentials of 10 applicants for a marketing representative position. Three of the applicants were Black and qualified for the position, two were qualified Whites, and five were unqualified Whites. (Qualifications were perceived as intended, based upon ratings provided by an independent sample not given information about applicant race.) Subjects were randomly assigned to an experimental condition in which a business justification to discriminate was supplied or to a control condition with no such justification. The justification informed subjects that the position applicants were to be considered for was in an all-White marketing team who served a White customer population. Moreover, they were told it was the practice of the professor's client to match the characteristic of marketing representatives to those of their customers. The dependent variables, discriminatory behavior, was measured by how many of three applicants recommended to be interviewed were Black; the fewer the number of Blacks, the more discrimination. Reizenstein and Brief observed a statistically significant interaction between modern racism scores and justification condition such that the greater the degree of which subjects harbored modern racist attitudes, the more they discriminate against Black applicants when provided with a justification. The researchers also depicted the interaction of dichotomizing subjects based upon their modern racism scores and reporting the number of Black applicants recommended by high and low prejudice subjects for each condition. In the justification condition, low prejudice subjects recommended an average of 1.10 Blacks, while high prejudice subjects recommended an average of only 0.53 Blacks. The average of the high prejudice subjects indicates they often selected an unqualified White over a qualified Black. The average number of Blacks chosen in the control condition was almost identical for low and high prejudice subjects.

Thus, the findings of Reizenstein and Brief (1995) are strongly supportive of our arguments. Importantly, their results have been "constructively replicated" (Lykken, 1968) by Pugh, Brief & Vaslow (1996). Collectively, these findings suggest that organizations may be populated with at least some Whites who unconsciously harbor negative attitudes towards Blacks. Indeed, these Whites view racism as bad and only act on their negative attitudes when provided with an excuse that protects them from being seem by themselves and others as racists. The excuses required for them to act, however, are seemingly commonplace, business justification to discriminate. Given these albeit preliminary but enlightening results, we now demonstrate their usefulness by turning to examples of recent investigations of workplace race relations in which explicit examination of the modern racism construct would have been informative.

RE-INTERPRETING THE DIVERSITY LITERATURE

Modern racism has yet to be measured in any field study comprising the limited empirical literature on diversity in organizations. Nevertheless, this literature provides examples suggestive of the gains that could be made if we were to take the theory of modern racism seriously. We begin with a study of Ibarra (1995), who investigated the effects of race on minority and White middle-level managers' informal job-related contracts in four large corporations. Ibarra observed a trend towards minority managers having fewer intimate network relationships than did their White counterparts. She attributed this trend to minorities also having more cross-race relationships than Whites. Such an attribution implies that the relationship minorities have with Whites are more distant than close. Why do these relationships lack closeness? A simple answer, yet one not considered by Ibarra, is that at least some of the Whites involved in job-related relationships with minorities may harbor unconscious, negative racial attitudes that preclude the development of close interpersonal relationships with Blacks. Consistent with the possibility that such negative attitudes are of the sort held by modern racists is the fact that she also observed Whites having more same-race relationships than did minorities. Therefore, the modern racism argument is evident in two ways. First, White network members of the minority manager may have kept their racial attitudes in check, with no business justifications to discriminate being evident, except as captured by Ibarra's subtle intimacy measure tapping the closeness of relationships. Second, some Whites may have exhibited their discomfort with minorities by choosing not to associate with them at all. Of course, since neither justification or racial attitudes were measured, our interpretation is speculative. Yet, the idea that a new kind of racism played a role in the pattern of findings Ibarra detected seems imminently plausible.

Racial attitudes seem to play an unrecognized role in another study of managerial networks. Hayes (1995) observed that corporate minority managers whose sets of job-related contacts were relatively integrated racially experienced lower rates of promotion than did minorities with largely White contacts. Again, the question is why? She explains this finding as supportive of a social capital perspective (i.e., its who you know that counts) (e.g., Coleman, 1986). But, let us probe a little deeper. Why are minorities who interact with other minorities organizationally disadvantaged? Might it be that their pattern of interactions is seen by modern racists as a legitimate concern to be taken into consideration in evaluating their promotability. That is, these minorities may be seen as not knowing the "right types of people" necessary to perform well at higher organizational levels. But, since we do not know either the racial attitudes of the decision makers in the financial services organization that hosted Hayes' research or how they, in fact, viewed that racial make-up of a promotion candidate's network, our interpretation, once again, remains speculative but plausible.

A close cousin of modern racism, "aversive racism" (Messick & Mackie, 1989), was evoked but not measured by the researchers who conducted our last exemplary diversity study. Tsui, Egan and O'Reilly (1992) found, as they predicted, that, for Whites, being increasingly racially different from others in one's work unit is related to lower levels of organizational attachment; and, for nonwhites, the relationship did not hold. Tsui et al's prediction was based on the reasoning that Whites who harbor negative racial attitudes may hold their racist behaviors in check and, alternatively, express their unease with minority co-workers by physically or psychologically withdrawing. We fully concur with Tsui et al's *a priori* thinking. Indeed, we applaud it. But, for the final time, we wish White racial attitudes were measured so as to ascertain if they, in fact, moderated the relationship between increasing minority work unit membership and attachment levels among Whites.

The above examples were selected, in part, because each of them is a methodologically sound study based on insightful theoretical reasoning. Nevertheless, we contend their findings suggest the need to attend directly to racial attitudes in the study of workplace race relations. The particular attitudes we advocate examining are those of the modern racist. It seems that it has become somewhat taboo to recognize the role of racism in contemporary American work organizations (as evidenced by the lack of research in this area). This taboo may be consistent with the current political and social climate in the United States. While such consistency may explain why racial attitudes currently are not a direct object of study in the organizations sciences, it in no way justifies the neglect.

EXTENDING THE BOUNDARIES OF DIVERSITY RESEARCH

We have argued that (a) racial discrimination in the employment arena remains an enduring problem in America; (b) the theory of modern racism (e.g., McConahay, 1986) and the concept of commonplace business justification to discriminate are useful tools for analyzing this problem; yet, (c) the direct study of racial attitudes and the contexts that stimulate their behavioral manifestations generally are ignored in the organizational sciences. We close this chapter by suggesting the sorts of research questions that ought to be pursued if the boundaries of organizational diversity studies are to be extended in ways likely to yield greater insights to the problem of employment discrimination and to its solutions.

Based upon the research of Ibarra (1995), Hayes (1995), and others, we know social networks are an empirically useful way of approaching diversity issues in organizations. How do the racial attitudes of a Black organizational members' White superiors, peers, and subordinates affect the characteristics of his/her network? One would not necessarily expect main effects for those attitudes, if they are of the modern racism sort. Rather, racial attitudes—network characteristics relationships should be evident primarily when the organizational context supplies a plausible, nonprejudiced explanation for what otherwise might be considered prejudiced behavior. What specific kinds of justification could cause a White, harboring modern racist attitudes, to distance him/herself from a Black co-worker? Might one be the belief that the Black would be more comfortable and otherwise better-off interacting with his/her "own kind". Lefkowitz's (1994) findings of racial segregation in the workplace certainly would suggest the plausibility of this belief. In addition to pursuing the influence of racial attitudes on network characteristics, questions about how those attitudes could possibly affect the influence of networks on the outcomes Blacks experience also seem important. For instance, recall our interpretation of Hayes' findings regarding the effects of networks on promotion rates. In sum, modern racism theory may help explain both the origins and functions of social networks in the workplace; but, for it to do so requires that racial attitudes be measured.

The relational demography framework used by, Egan & O'Reilly (1992) has contributed much to the understanding of diversity in organizations. (Also see Tsui, Egan and Xin (1995)). However, to move beyond the mere observation that relational measures are associated with important outcomes requires deeper probing. Are modern racist attitudes an explanation for Whites being relatively less attached to racially integrated work units? Taking a step back, do those attitudes influence the degree to which a unit becomes integrated? How might the *distribution* of modern racist attitudes in a unit affect both scores on relational measures of organizational demography and the correlates of those scores? Is it the unit head's racial attitudes that count or the attitudes shared within the unit?

More generally, we need to learn more about the variety and prevalence of business justification to discriminate. Are these justifications themselves a product of modern racists' attitudes or simply a reflection of economic reasoning? In addition, it is important to learn if organizations populated by modern racists attract like-minded persons, as suggested by Schneider's (1987) attraction–selection–attrition model. Perhaps the most pressing question to be addressed is, "Can organizations modify the racial attitudes of its members?" What kind of policies, practices and/or procedures are required to affect such a change? Finally, until we know how the attitudes of a modern racist might be modified, what can organizations do to keep those attitudes from becoming behaviorally manifest?

We are sure the above questions merely represent the tip of those that should be unearthed. We also are sure that racial discrimination in America exists and that it can only be understood fully by the direct examination of racial attitudes, like modern racism. But, Black Americans are far from the only victims of discrimination in the workplace. Women, both in the United States and elsewhere, also are too often victimized at work. Recently, Swim et al. (1995) have applied the ideas behind modern racism to understand the treatment of women, defining the construct of "modern sexism". It may be the case that the victimization of groups, no matter their geographical location, can be understood better by examining the ways in which the larger political and social context in which those groups are embedded has modified the relationship between attitudes and discriminatory behaviors. That is, as blatant forms of racism become unacceptable in the United States, so too may have other blatantly negative attitudes towards other groups in other cultures become altered. Such alterations would mean that attitudes toward a group (e.g., Protestants attitudes towards Catholics in Northern Ireland) will not necessarily predict behaviors towards the group; to act against the group might require a plausible, nonprejudiced justification (e.g., "Our Protestant customer base won't buy from a Catholic"). Thus, the ideas and arguments we have presented here may be applicable, with modifications, to understanding the victimization of various stigmatized groups around the world.

SUMMARY

In this chapter, we have argued (a) racial discrimination in the employment area remains an enduring problem in the United States; (b) the theory of modern racism (e.g., McConahay, 1986) and the concept of "commonplace business justifications to discriminate" are useful tools for analyzing this problem; yet, (c) the direct study of racial attitudes and the contexts that stimulate their behavioral manifestations generally have been ignored in the organizational sciences. In light of these arguments, a re-interpretation of the diversity literature is provided; and, explicit suggestions for extending the boundaries of that literature are supplied. These suggestions recognize that Black Americans are far from the only victims of employment discrimination.

REFERENCES

Banaji, M. R. & Greenwald, A. G. (1994) Implicit stereotyping and unconscious prejudice. In M. P. Zanna & J. M. Olson (Eds.), *The psychology of prejudice, The Ontario Symposium*, Vol. 7, pp. 55–76. Hillsdale, NJ: Erlbaum.
Barnard, C. I. (1938) *The Functions of the Executive.* Cambridge, MA: Harvard University Press.
Baritz, L. (1960) *The Servants of Power—A History of the Use of Social Science in American Industry.* Middletown, CT: Wesleyan University Press.
Bendick, M. Jr., Jackson, C. W. & Reinoso, V. A. (1994) Measuring employment discrimination through controlled experiments. *Review of Black Political Economy*, **23**, 25–48.
Blauner, B. (1989) *Black Lives, White Lives: Three Decades of Race Relations in America.* Berkeley: University of California Press.
Bowen, D. E., Ledford, G. E. & Nathan, B. N. (1991) Hiring for the organization, not the job. *Academy of Management Executive*, **5**, 35–51.
Braham, J. (1987) Is the door really open? *Industry Week*, November 64–70.
Brief, A. P., Buttram, R. T., Elliott, J. D., Reizenstein, R. M. & McCline, R. L. (1995)

Releasing the beast: A study of compliance with orders to use race as a selection criterion. *Journal of Social Issues*, **51**, 177–193.

Coleman, J. S. (1986) Social theory, social research, and a theory of action, *American Journal of Sociology*, **94**, 95–120.

Cox, T., Jr. (1993) *Cultural Diversity in Organizations: Theory, Research, and Practice*. San Francisco: Berrett-Koehler.

Cox, T., Jr.& Blake, S. (1991) Managing cultural diversity: Implications for organizational competitiveness. *The Executive*, **5**, 45–56.

Cox, T. & Nkomo, S. M. (1990) Invisible men and women: A status report on race as a variable in organization behavior research. Journal of Organizational Behavior, **11**, 419–431.

Crosby, F., Bromley, S. & Saxe, L. (1980) Recent unobtrusive studies of black and white discrimination and prejudice: A literature review. *Psychological Bulletin*, **87**, 546–563.

Dovidio, J. F. & Gaertners, S. L. (1991) Changes in the nature and assessment of racial prejudice. In H. Knopke, J. Norrell & R. Rodgers (Eds.), *Opening doors: An Appraisal of Race Relations in Contemporary America*, pp. 201–241. Tuscaloosa: University of Alabama Press.

Essed, P. (1991) *Everyday racism*. Newbury Park, CA: Sage.

Gaertner, S. L. (1976) Nonreactive measures in racial attitude research: A focus on "Liberals". In P. A. Katz (Ed.), *Towards the Elimination of Racism*. New York: Pergamon Press.

Gaertner, S. L. & Dovidio, J. F. (1981) Racism among the well intentioned. In J. Bermingham & E. Claussen (Eds.), *Racism, Pluralism and Public Policy: A Search for Equality*. Boston: G. K. Hall.

Greeley, A. M. & Sheatsley, P. B. (1971) Attitudes toward racial integration. *Scientific American*, **225**, 13–19.

Hayes, E. (1995) It's not what you know, it's who you know: The effects of human and social capital on race differences in promotion and support. Paper presented at the Academy of Management Meetings, Vancouver, British Columbia.

Ibarra, H. (1995) Race, opportunity, and diversity of social circles in managerial networks. *Academy of Management Journal*, **38**, 673–703.

Jensen, A. R. (1985) The nature of the black–white difference on various psychometric tests: Spearman's hypothesis. *Behavioral and Brain Sciences*, **8**, 193–263.

Jones, E. W. Jr. (1973) What it's like to be a black manager. *Harvard Business Review*, **51**, 108–116.

Kaplan, A. (1964) *The Conduct of Inquiry: Methodology for the Behavioral Sciences*. Scranton, PA: Chandler.

Katz, R. (1981) *Stigma: A Social–Psychological Analysis*. Hillsdale, NJ: Erblaum.

Kinder, D. R. (1986) The continuing American dilemma: White resistance to racial change 40 years after Mydral. *Journal of Social Issues*, **42**, 151–171.

Kinder, D. R. & Rhodebeck, L. A. (1982) Continuities in support for racial equality. *Public Opinion Quarterly*, **46**, 195–215.

Kinder, D. R. & Sears, D. (1981) Prejudice and politics: Symbolic racism versus threats to the good life. *Journal of Personality and Social Psychology*, **40**, 414–431.

Lefkowitz, J. (1994) Race as a factor in job placement: Serendipitous findings of "ethnic drift" *Personnel Psychology*, **47**, 497–513.

Lykken, D. T. (1968) Statistical significance in psychological research. *Psychological Bulletin*, **70**, 151–159.

McConahay, J. B. (1983) Modem racism and modem discrimination: The effects of race, racial attitudes, and context on stimulated hiring decisions. *Personality and Social Psychology Bulletin*, **9**, 551–558.

McConahay, J. B. (1986) Modern racism, ambivalence, and the modern racism scale. In J. Dovidio & S. Gaertner (Eds.), *Prejudice, Discrimination, and Racism*, pp. 91–124. New York: Academic Press.

McConahay, J. B., Hardee, B. B. & Batts, V. (1981) Has racism declined? It depends upon who's asking and what is asked. *Journal of Conflict Resolution*, **2**, 563–579.

Messick, D. M. & Mackie, D. M. (1989) Intergroup relations. In M. R. Rosenweig & L. W. Porter (Eds.), *Annual Review of Psychology*, **40**, 45–81. Palo Alto, CA: Annual Reviews.

Myrdal, G. (1944) *An American Dilemma: The Negro Problem and Modern Democracy*. New York: Harper and Row.

Nkomo, S. M. (1992) The emperor has no clothes: Rewriting race in organizations. *Academy of Management Review*, **17**, 487–513.

Nord, W. R. (1977) Job satisfaction reconsidered. *American Psychologist*, **32**, 1026–1035.

Pugh, S. D., Brief, A. P. & Vaslow, J. B. (1996) *Prejudicial Hiring Practices: The Roles of Authority, Legitimacy and Modern Racism*. Paper presented at the Academy of Management Meetings, Cincinnati, OH.

Rawls, J. (1971) *A Theory of Justice*. Cambridge, MS: Harvard University Press.

Reizenstein, R. M. & Brief, A. P. (1995) *Just Doing Business: Compliance and Racism as Explanations for Unfair Employment Discrimination*. Paper presented at the American Psychological Society, New York.

Schneider, B. (1987) The people make the place. *Personnel Psychology*, **14**, 437–453.

Sears, D. O. (1988) Symbolic racism. In P.A. Katz & D. A. Taylor (Eds.), *Eliminating racism*, pp. 53–84. New York: Plenum Press.

Sears, D. O. & Allen, H. M., Jr.(1984) The trajectory of local desegregation controversies and whites opposition to busing. In N. Miller & M. B. Brewer (Eds.), *Groups in Contact: The Psychology of Desegregation*, pp. 123–157. Orlando, FL: Academic Press.

Sears, D. O., Hensler, C. P. & Speer, L. K. (1979) Whites' opposition to "busing". Self interest or symbolic politics? *American Political Science Review*, **73**, 369–384.

Smith, T. W. & Sheatsley, P. B. (1984) American attitudes towards race relations. *Public Opinion*, 14–15, 50–53.

Sniderman, P. M. & Tetlock, P. E. (1986) Symbolic racism: Problems of motive attribution in political analysis. *Journal of Social Issues*, **42**, 129–150.

Sniderman, P. M., Piazza, T., Tetlock, P. E. & Kendrick, A. (1991) The new racism. *American Journal of Political Science*, **35**, 423–447.

Stone, E. F., Stone, D. L. & Dipboye, R. L. (1992) Stigmas in organizations: Race, handicaps, and physical unattractiveness. In K. Kelley (Ed.), *Issues, Theory, and Research in Industrial/Organizational Psychology*. Amsterdam, Holland: Elsevier Science.

Swim, J. K., Aikin, K. J., Hall, W. S. & Hunter, B. A. (1995) Sexism & Racism: old fashioned and modern prejudices. *Journal of Personality and Social Psychology*, **68**, 199–214.

Taylor, D. G., Sheatsley, P. B. & Greeley, A. M. (1978) Attitudes toward racial integration. *Scientific American*, **238**, 42–51.

Tsui, A. S., Egan, T. D. & O'Reilly, C. A. (1992) Being different: Relational demography and organizational attachment. *Administrative Science Quarterly*, **37**, 549–579.

Tsui, A. S., Egan, T. D. & Xin, K. R. (1995) Diversity in organizations: Lessons from demography research. In M. Chemers, S. Oskamp & M. Costanzo (Eds.), *Diversity in Organizations*. Thousand Oaks: Sage Publications.

Van Dijk, T. A. (1987) *Communicating Racism: Ethnic Prejudice in Thought and Talk*. Newbury Park, CA: Sage.

Watkins, S. (1993) Racism du jour at Shoney's. *The Nation*, October, 424–427.

White, K. R. (1982) The relation between socioeconomic status and academic achievement. *Psychological Bulletin*, **91**, 461–481.

CHAPTER 8

New Facets of Commitment in Response to Organizational Change: Research Trends and the Dutch Experience

René Schalk and Charissa Freese
Work and Organizational Research Centre (WORC), Tilburg University

The last decades have been turbulent for organizations throughout the industrialized world. Organizations are confronted with many changes in their environment, caused by processes like an intensified global competition, the decline of industry and growth of the service sector, new developments in technology and increasing customer demands, as well as shorter life cycles of products and services.

To meet the increasing demands of the unpredictable environment in which organizations operate, the keyword for organizations has become "change", which often means downsizing and reframing the organization, restructuring jobs and work processes. These developments have consequences for employees, and imply that work relationships are changing (McLean Parks & Kidder, 1994). Often, employment relationships have to be re-established (Sugalski, Manzo & Meadows, 1995), which means changing the "deal" even when keeping the people (Rousseau, 1996a).

The "old deal" between employer and employee, which was based on the straightforward exchange of job security and material rewards for loyalty, does not seem to fit the current situation in many organizations, and needs to be replaced by a "new deal" in which organizations and employees come to a renewed agreement about their mutual obligations in the light of changing circumstances.

Trends in Organizational Behavior, Volume 4. Edited by C. L. Cooper and D. M. Rousseau.
© 1997 John Wiley & Sons Ltd.

But how will such a "new deal" look like? This depends, of course, on the new reality in the workplace, which may even be the context of a virtual organizations (Davidow & Malone, 1992; Jackson & Van der Wielen, in press), a jobless organization (Bridges, 1994), or a continuously changing organization implying uncertainty (Handy, 1995).

An ideal new employment deal would be a win–win agreement based on clarified mutual expectations, based on mutual responsibility between employees and employers, leading to mutual understanding and commitment, and improved organizational effectiveness (Covey, 1994).

Maintaining commitment is a crucial issue in situations of creating new employment deals. Because commitment is linked to the behavior of employees in their work (service, citizenship, learning, attendance) employers will probably prefer to maintain commitment of their employees when changing the deal. But at the same time employers may alter the nature of expected commitment. For example, employers might like to maintain a high level of affective commitment, but to avoid too high levels of continuance commitment to increase mobility. Also new forms of commitment might emerge as important in creating new employment deals.

A recent study in the United Kingdom (Kessler & Undy, 1996) provides evidence that some employers are indeed actively seeking to define and develop a new understanding with their employees, especially with respect to the key areas of the employment relationship: reward, job security and culture. Examples of this are introducing more fluid, flexible and less differentiated pay structures, more individualized pay systems, giving guarantees of job security or preparing people through training and development for future employment, introducing programs for culture change (from producer-orientation to customer-orientation, from employee/manager divisiveness to a "shared" approach) (Kessler & Undy, 1996, pp. 29–33).

However, in many firms a gap remains between the loyalty of employees and the trust which they have in top management (Kessler & Undy, 1996). This means that if employers believe that they can ease the effects of, for example, lay-offs and restructuring of the organization by imposing a new deal on the employees, which will automatically result in a renewed psychological contract with their employees, this is refuted by reality (Pickard, 1995). The human resource challenge of the 1990s is to manage the effective implementation of new deals, which means changing the psychological contract (Guzzo & Noonan & Elron, 1994; Rousseau & Greller, 1994; Sims, 1994; Hiltrop, 1995; Rousseau, 1996a).

In this chapter we will go into two subjects which relate to the implementation of new deals, and the consequences that this may have, seen from a psychological contract perspective. Changes in psychological contracts may have implications for employee attitude and behavior, especially organizational commitment. We will discuss how commitment is related to changes in the psychological contract. We will take the relay baton from McLean Parks and Kidder (1994) who in their chapter on "Changing work relationships in the 1990s" posed the question, "What happens when the psychological contract is kept?", and, "Can, once violated, a psychological contract be healed?".

We argue that in addition to gradual increases of commitment when contracts are fulfilled changes in organizational commitment may also result from revisions of the relationship between employer and employee. Further, we maintain that there is not in all situations a linear, continuous relationship between the psychological contract and commitment, but that contract violations or exceeding of expectations may lead to sudden revisions or abandonment of the contract. New deals can only promote commitment and organizational effectiveness, under conditions supporting both organizational and individual needs. We propose a framework specifying the change process.

THE RELATIONSHIP BETWEEN THE PSYCHOLOGICAL CONTRACT AND COMMITMENT

Psychological contracts develop from beliefs when the individual employee believes there is an obligation to give certain contributions in exchange for particular inducements. Contracts are perceptions of mutual obligations and not mere expectations (Rousseau, 1990). Therefore, the existence of a psychological contract implies that the employee is willing to accept work roles and tasks offered by the organization, and to carry them out in accordance to certain standards.

Although contracts are by definition accepted voluntary agreements between parties to do something (Rousseau & McLean, Parks, 1993), the terms of the agreed contract may be more or less in convergence with an employees' needs and expectations. If the contract is accepted by an employee this implies that he or she is willing to follow through with these terms. However, the contract will be perceived by the employee as more favorable or more unfavorable to him/herself. That is, the employee evaluates the actual "state of affairs" with respect to the mutual obligations between employer and employee compared to his or her needs and expectations. More favorable terms for the employee will probably lead to a more favorable perception of the organization and greater commitment to the relationship.

Thus, the perception of (un)favorableness influences organizational commitment, and consequently the readiness to accept work roles and tasks, the willingness to engage in extra-role behaviors, and the willingness to avoid negative behaviors such as coming in late and not performing well. Dutch research shows that a more favorable psychological contract is related to a higher degree of organizational commitment (Freese & Schalk, 1996). The degree of commitment may also change in response to certain events in the work domain. For example, in a study in which 40 employees of an Australian organization offering telecommunication services were interviewed (Campbell, 1995) it was found that 90% were able to describe a negative and/or positive critical incident in their career. The nature of the negative incidents, where positive expectations were disappointed, concerned events such as the quality of working material, and relocations, payrises, promotions or changes of position that were not granted. Positive unexpected incidents included getting surprise bonuses, vouchers or awards, positive working outcomes, customer satisfaction, promotions or payrises. These incidents were considered by 40% as having had a great impact on their attitudes towards their work and the organization.

However, in our view there is not a continuous (linear) relationship between the psychological contract and commitment. An employees' commitment may remain relatively stable over time, in spite of evident variations in the exchange relationship between the organization and the individual, but may then show a sudden drop under circumstances perceived as critical by the employee.

The psychological contract includes beliefs about what falls within the boundaries of acceptability and what is absolutely intolerable in the interaction with the organization. These boundaries of what is perceived as acceptable and tolerable by employees with respect to reciprocal obligations should be taken into account to explain changes and consequences of changes in psychological contracts.

Employees who believe that the organization has overstepped the boundaries of their psychological contract (contract violation) will be more likely to have high levels of tardiness, absenteeism, and intention to leave the organization (Cartwright & Cooper, 1994; Robinson, Kraatz & Rousseau, 1994; Robinson & Rousseau, 1994).

To explain the dynamic processes of changes in the psychological contract and, particularly the features of sudden change, Roe & Schalk (1996) have proposed a model, that assumes that the employee observes the actual behavior of the organization and him/herself and compares this with the behavior to be expected on the basis of the psychological contract. The model is based on a distinction between aspects considered as basic values in work by the employee and aspects considered as important within the framework of an existing psychological contract.

The distinction between the evaluation of (violations of) the existing contract and basic values is reflected in different boundaries in Roe & Schalk's model, which will be elaborated later in this chapter. First we will go into the process of evaluation of the existing psychological contract.

Roe and Schalk's model states that the employee compares the actual behavior of the organization and his or her own behavior with what would be expected on the basis of the psychological contract. This means that the employee monitors and evaluates whether deviations from agreed upon mutual obligations within the framework of the existing psychological contract occur. In the case of minor deviations the employee may take corrective actions without changing the psychological contract. In the case of major deviations, the employee will take corrective actions as well, but these actions result in a change of the psychological contract. The psychological contract serves as a cognitive model of monitoring behavior, and remains in use as a basis for action, until it becomes clear to the employee (for example from unexpected events or by a gradual drift which leads to critical boundaries being overstepped) that it has lost its validity, which means that the contract no longer holds in the individual's thinking due to change or revision.

An illustration of this process is the following citation from an interview with an older employee of the former Volvo car manufacturing plant in the Netherlands, employed in a department that offers employment for employees with disabilities.

> I was ill for a lot of time, and experienced lots of stress; the group fell apart, and did get split up; I felt like an outsider. I got older, I don't feel at home anymore in the new production line of the cars. (Freese & Schalk, 1995).

The situation this employee was confronted with was the following. He was for many years employed in the production line of a certain type of car. Then the plant stopped producing these cars, and started to produce another model, with a new production line. Working on the new production line required special skills of employees to be acquired through additional training. The chances to successfully complete the training were assessed as being too low for a number of (mainly unskilled) employees, for whom other (low-level) jobs inside or outside the organization were sought. This employee was, because of his absenteeism rate, his age and his skills, removed from the production line, which also meant for him losing the opportunity to maintain social relationships at work with his colleagues from his former workgroup. This made him realize that his "old" contract has lost its validity.

The psychological contract as a cognitive model is in normal circumstances balanced (Rousseau, 1995), i.e. in a state of homeostasis.

This model serves as a frame of reference, from which it is easier to evaluate what happens in the work domain (cognitive ease). People will try to match events into this scheme as long as it has not apparently lost its validity. The contract model is applicable to a certain range of acceptable experiences, in other words there is a "zone of acceptance" (Rousseau, 1995).

The "change" model of the psychological contract (Roe & Schalk, 1996) is presented in Figure 8.1. According to Roe & Schalk (1996) the behavior of the organization and the employee (as perceived by the employee) vary over time, with fluctuations within a certain range. For example, the employee may work harder, be more helpful to colleagues, or perform more effectively on certain days than on others, while the conditions at work or the support of the supervisor fluctuate as well over time. The psychological contract allows for such changes, at least within certain limits. There is a band of acceptable variation with an upper and lower acceptability limit, as well as a band of tolerable variation with an upper and lower tolerance limit.

The boundaries of what is considered as acceptable are determined by the aspects considered as important within the framework of the existing psychological contract. What is considered as tolerable variation is determined by the basic values of the individual employee, regardless the framework of the existing contract.

To clarify this distinction we will give some figures about aspects people value in work from longitudinal studies of the Dutch

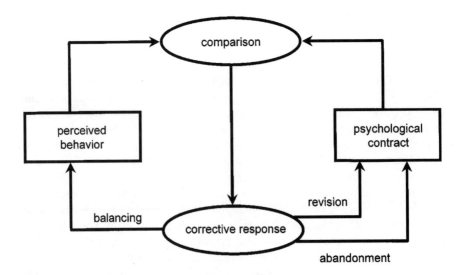

Figure 8.1 "Change" model of the psychological contract

Organization for Labor Market Research (OSA) based on interviews with a representative sample of the Dutch working population. These figures show that the aspect that people rank first in importance when they would have to look for another job is Interesting Work (1985: 46%, 1988: 47%), followed by Good Income (1985: 25%, 1988: 24%), Security (1985: 13%, 1988: 10%) and Good Contacts with Others (1985: 9%, 1988: 11%), Future Job Prospects (1985: 6%, 1988: 7%) and Good Supervisor (1985: 1%, 1988: 2%). The figures were very much the same in 1985 and 1988. In 1992 the question was asked what people valued in their work, and Interesting Work was considered by 47% as very important, Good Contacts and Others was very important for 45%, Good Supervisor for 36%, Future Job Prospects for 26%, Security for 32%, and Good Income for 27%.

Although there is a striking difference between the figure of 1985/1988 on the one hand and those of 1992 on the other hand, this does not necessarily mean that there has been a radical shift in the work values of the Dutch working population. A more plausible explanation is that different questions were asked. In 1985/1988 it was asked, "What would be most important if you were looking for a job?". In 1992 it was asked how important employees valued a number of aspects in their current job situation.

The differences in answers to these questions are likely to illustrate that what people indicate to be important is determined by the way in which choices are framed. Features of the current job (evaluated within the framework of an existing psychological contract) are valued differently than when a hypothetical new job is considered (reflecting basic aspects people value in work).

When contracts are agreed upon they will always fall within the tolerable variation determined by basic values. Employees will not voluntarily accept contract terms violating their basic values. When basic values are at stake in the work situation, for example when practices considered as obligatory in a religious context are prohibited, or when the work environment becomes too dangerous or threatening, the boundaries of tolerable variation will be considered as being overstepped.

Specific contracts include a zone of acceptance of variation between acceptability limits, that reflect what the employee feels is acceptable variation within the agreed contract terms. For example, with regard to feedback from the supervisor, an employee may expect weak or moderate praise or criticism (within acceptability limits); strong praise or criticism may be found unexpected or not in agreement with the framework of the existing psychological contract (beyond acceptability, within tolerance limits) or intolerable, violating an employees' basic values (beyond tolerance limits).

Dutch research (e.g. Schouten, 1994; De Bot, 1996) shows that negative deviations from the status quo are reported more often than positive deviations. This indicates that people may have lower tolerance for negative than positive boundaries, or that negative deviations are more easily recalled. Roe & Schalk (1996) describe three typical patterns of variations in organizational and individual behavior. Variations in the perceived behavior of the organization and/or the individual that remain within the acceptance limits are without consequences for the psychological contract, and thus for commitment, and subsequent behavior. Positive deviations of the organization's behavior are likely to be followed by positive deviations on the individual side, while negative deviations would have the opposite effect. This pattern is called *balancing*.

If the perceived behavior of the organization and/or the individual reaches or exceeds the acceptability levels, changes in consequences are expected. In this case one would expect the person to reconsider the contract as well as to show a decline in commitment, and subsequent behaviors (Kotter, 1973). Furthermore, clarification about the re-negotiation of the contract is to be expected. This pattern is called *revision*, as it may lead to a revised contract. When the deviation is above the tolerance limits the contract is likely to break down. Accordingly, one may expect commitment to drop strongly, and behavioral responses to be extreme. Open conflicts, emotional expressions, and signs of aggression and depression may occur as well (Rousseau, 1990). This condition is called *abandonment* by Roe & Schalk (1996). Schouten (1994) did in-depth interviews with a random sample of 27 employees in which he, among other things, asked them whether it had occurred in their career in the organization by that they expected something of the organization which didn't happen. He also asked if anything did happen which they hadn't expected. We will give some quotations from these interviews as examples of the processes of balancing, revision and abandonment.

When no unexpected negative or positive event occurs the psychological contract is in homeostatis, which means that balancing would be the expected process in reaction to minor changes. Thirteen employees (48%) did not report negative incidents, and seventeen (63%) did not report positive incidents. Fourteen employees reported negative incidents, most of them related to not getting a promotion or another job. Ten employees reported positive incidents, mostly unexpected rewards or bonuses or a promotion or job change. Reactions to negative incidents were often more explicitly worded ("I was angry, disappointed, I did try to do something about it") than reactions to positive incidents.

Examples of a balancing process are:

In the past I did apply for the job of head of the department of domestic affairs, but unfortunately they hired someone else. Although he had a longer period of tenure in this organization, it was a disappointment for me. My reaction was anger: Why him? I did this work for a long time, and he didn't. But I didn't do anything afterwards, because they had chosen him already [female, deputy head department of domestic affairs].

I came from a secretarial job into a personnel consultant's role when the organization was growing. I had followed an education for that and did get offered this new job. My tasks would be expanded and I would get a higher salary. However, this took a long time, and I did get very angry, but mainly disappointed. My reaction has been, anyway, to do something about it, and I did make this clear. It gives one the opportunity to develop autonomy and assertiveness [female, personnel consultant].

In the transformation process of the organization, a long time ago, new heads of department had to be appointed. I was deputy head at that moment and did get offered a department. That was for my age at that time rather unexpected. It was kind of an acknowledgement for me [male, head R&D department].

The difference between balancing and revision is, that in a revision process the way of thinking about the contract changes, whereas in balancing the contract remains the same. Only longitudinal research assessing the content of the psychological contract at different points in time will be able to reveal processes of revision. From interviewing employees about experiences with critical incidents after they have occurred it is hard to assess whether a revision or balancing process has taken place.

The following quotation seems to illustrate a revision process, because the employee involved did not get a job he applied for, resulting in a loss of motivation. He then re-evaluated his relationship with the organization, probably developed a revised contract, adjusting the boundaries of what was acceptable, and did get motivated again. Eventually he did even get the job he wanted to have.

The first time I applied for the job of deputy head they turned me down. That was a disappointment, and this has consequences for the way you do your work. But then I have tried by means of conversations with the department head to analyze what had happened and then I did get motivated again to perform well. Later on it turned out that the decision of the organization did make sense. One year later I did get the opportunity again and then they hired me [male, absenteeism counsellor].

Examples of abandonment:

At a certain moment I had certain task which I did with pleasure. By organizational restructuring I was forced to change jobs to another department, with other tasks. I could not identify with these tasks. After a long period of habituation, it turned out that my affection for my previous work was so strong that I could not get interested enough in this work. This resulted in lower effort and activity. In spite of conversations about this and promises being made, nothing ever came out of this. Then you still have this bitter taste [male, bank employee].

I was in a situation in which I had great responsibility. I was the second man in the department, after the department head. I had the feeling that I did a lot of the supervisory tasks of the department, certainly with respect to technical matters. However, the salary offered for this in comparison with other comparable jobs was in my view too low. The organization said that they couldn't do anything about that. That was the trigger for me to try to find another job... [male, accountancy employee].

Models of balancing, revision and abandonment are given in Figures 8.2, 8.3 and 8.4. As long as new deals don't overstep the boundaries of what individuals consider as acceptable the psychological contract remains balanced, with no detrimental effects on commitment. New demands made by the employer are then in line with the employees' expectations about mutual obligations. When a new deal oversteps the

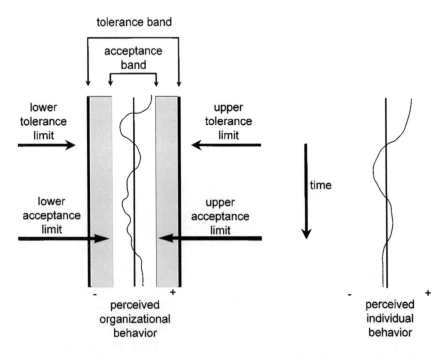

Figure 8.2 Perceived behavior and acceptance and tolerance limits of the psychological contract: balancing

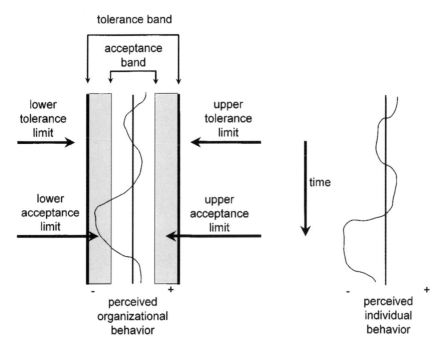

Figure 8.3 Perceived behavior and acceptance and tolerance limits of the psychological contract: revision

boundaries of acceptance, which might also result from a gradual cognitive drift or contract drift (Rousseau, 1995) a critical phase is entered. The outcome of this may be a revision of the psychological contract or abandonment of the contract.

If both the employer and the employee agree that revision would be the preferred outcome (changing the deal while keeping the people), an organization and employee have to negotiate about what the new deal and revised psychological contract will look like. A revision may succeed when employees feel that new demands are imposed by the employer, but that they also get something in return that fulfils their needs. Also in situations when the organization is able to justify the change of the deal to the employees a revision may succeed. For example, employees of an organization may accept a lower salary, if there is a chance that this may provide a solution for financial problems of the organization, which would improve their chances of keeping their job. This happened in the Fokker aviation company in the Netherlands.

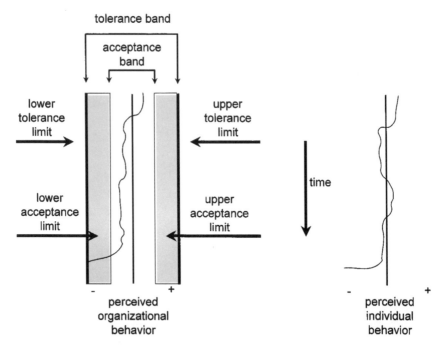

Figure 8.4 Perceived behavior and acceptance and tolerance limits of the psychological contract: abandonment

To make a revision succeed, an organization has to look for what it can offer to an employee and the employee what he or she can accept so that the organization and employee create a new balanced psychological contract.

WHAT ARE THE NEW DEALS THAT CAN WORK?

Although employees' psychological contracts are influenced by the situation the organizational faces, this does not imply that new deals can be implemented without problems in critical situations. New deals can only work when there is a mutual benefit for both parties. This means that one-sided new deals imposed by employer which do not comply with individual values and expectations are doomed to fail.

This can be illustrated with the findings of Dutch research, which tried to find out whether there were "new employees" to fit into the general model employers have about a new deal. According to the authors of this study (De Korte & Bolweg, 1994), based on what is written in the media, on the literature and in ideas of employers and organizations of employers, the new employees are supposed to be individualistic, to be not closely tied to the employer, to be calculating job-hoppers, to be very well educated, to be demanding, to think they know better, to be mobile, to be flexible, committed, and to belonging to such categories as the yuppy (young urban professional), the dinky (double income, no kids), the yiffy (young, individualistic, freedom-minded, few) or the lime'r (less income, more excitement).

Contrasting this with idea, De Korte & Bolweg's (1994) data of in depth interviews with specific groups of employees where you might expect to find new employees (13 young professionals in the law, 15 economists and 16 sales people in banks, 14 chemical process operators and 20 retail sales employees) reveal that workers' deals do not conform to the employer's stereotype. Instead, characteristics of the "real new employees" included that they are social, in the sense that they consider their working relationship as important, that they are attached to their team or work group (cohesive, willing to stand in if necessary), that they consider career prospects and opportunities as important, that they aim for security, that they have a high need for autonomy, and that they want attention from management (particularly genuine interest from management in what employees are doing).

Another example can be derived from a study on differences in psychological contracts between part-time and full-time employees (Schalk, Van den Bosch & Freese, 1994). In this study, among female employees and supervisors working part-time, the expectations regarding personal development were perceived as being less fulfilled by the organization than was the case with female or supervisory full-time employees.

That it is important to take social aspects of the job, opportunities for meeting other people and building good relationships into consideration was shown in a study of the introduction of a new planning system in a department store, where part-time employees showed a greater decline in job satisfaction than full-time employees (Freese & Schalk, 1996). The planning system not only resulted in different working hours, but also in variable breaks. This meant that employees would almost every day have breaks with different people. This made it harder for employees to build good relationships. Of course this was unpleasant for all employees, but the part-time employees were affected more deeply, because their main reason for working, the social aspects of their work, could no longer be fulfilled.

These examples illustrate the differences in psychological contracts, and clarifies why different groups of employees may respond differently to the same situation, depending on what they value in their jobs.

Often different perspectives are found in the workforce. For example, young people with little job experience might like to be offered extensive training, so they are able to find another job more easily. Older people might prefer more flexible and higher pension benefits, so they won't have to worry so much about their income after they retire. Part-time employees, who also take care of their children, working flexible hours, might need a day-care center that accepts children on variable hours and days (Freese & Schalk, 1996). Organizations could take this into account, for example, by offering choices from a certain variety of provisions, reflecting an intersection across the different employee perspectives.

In trying to create a new deals, organizations after screening out those employees whose values are widely at variance with the contract terms the organization can offer, could take differences in psychological contracts between different categories of employees into consideration by offering some variation in packages.

From Rousseau (1996b) we derive some examples of features of new deals that can work regarding career prospects for managerial and professional jobs. Important features might be offering choices and opportunities to participate in the design of the new employment arrangement, offering terms with value on the external market as well as the internal market, opportunities to apply abilities, skills, and knowledge to new markets, opportunities for cross-functional or inter-firm experiences, periodic re-skilling, opportunities for phased retirement and creating safety nets and supports to make employees less vulnerable.

Many organizations will have to work on communicating and implementing new deals with their employees. What may facilitate this process is that most employees do realize that, as a consequence of the changes in environment in organizations, job security can no longer be guaranteed. This is at least the case in the Netherlands where downsizing in such industrial organizations as Philips, Shell, DAF and Fokker has had much attention in the media, and government organizations and the service sector are also affected by this phenomenon. Changes in organizations have made employees aware of the fact that the economic situation nowadays implies that "the only thing that is certain is that things are not certain".

Most employees are willing to adjust their career expectations from "the organization should provide for my career" to "the organizational should provide for circumstances in which I can work on my own employability", if the employer indeed provides possibilities in this respect.

CONCLUSION

In this chapter we have described how commitment may change as a consequence of different patterns in the dynamics of psychological contracts, which also applies to situations in which a new deal has to be created. The creation of a totally new deal implies a fundamental revision of the psychological contract, in which a new balance has to be found in the ratio of inputs and outputs (Adams, 1965). For the organization as well as for the employee this means finding a new equilibrium in their mutual obligations. In the process of creating new deals with employees the challenge for human resources management is to balance new demands with provisions which fit in with the needs of employees. It is important to make the employment deal explicit to employees, with respect to what is expected of them and what they will get in return. The prime responsibility for clear new deals starts with the employer communicating on this issue. Not clearly communicating with employees may lead to violations of the psychological contract, overstepping the boundaries and abandonment of the contract, which will lead to low levels of commitment.

REFERENCES

Adams, J. S. (1965)E Inequity in social exchange. In L. Berkowitz (Ed.), *Advances in Experimental Social Psychology*, Vol. 2. New York: Academic.

Bridges, W. (1994) *JobShift: How to Prosper in a Workplace without Jobs*. Reading, Addison-Wesley.

Cambell, J. W. (1995) Organisational change and the psychological contract. Melbourne/Tilburg: Unpublished thesis work and organizational psychology, Tilburg University.

Cartwright, S. & Cooper, C.L. (1994) The human effects of mergers and acquisitions. In: Cooper, C. L. & Rousseau, D. M. (Eds.), *Trends in Organizational Behavior*. Vol. 1: John Wiley, p. 47–61.

Covey, S. (1994) Make it win-win. *Incentive*, **168**, 10, 16.

Davidow, W. H. & Malone, M. S. (1992) *The Virtual Corporation: Structuring and Revitalizing the Corporation for the 21st Century*. New York: Harper Business.

De Bot, M. (1996) The psychological contract of temporary and permanent employees: Contents and consequences. A Dutch study. Tilburg: Unpublished thesis work and organizational psychology, Tilburg University.

De Korte, A. W. & Bolweg, J. F. (1994) *De nieuwe werknemer?! [The new employee?!]*. Assen: Van Goreum.

Freese, C. & Schalk, R. (1995) Het psychologisch contract en leeftijdsbewust personeelmanagement [The psychological contract and age related HRM]. In: Schalk, R. (Ed.) *Oudere werknemers in een veranderende wereld [Older Employees in a Changing World]*. Utrecht: Lemma, p. 207–223.

Freese, C. & Schalk, R. (1996) Implications of differences in psychological contracts for human resources management. *European Journal of Work and organizational Psychology* (in press).

Guzzo, R. A. & Noonan, K. A. (1994) Human resource practices at communications and the psychological contract. *Human Resource Management,* **33,** 447–462.

Guzzo, R. A., Noonan, K. A. & Elron, E. (1994) Expatriate managers and the psychological contract. *Journal of Applied Psychology,* **79,** 617–626.

Handy, C. (1995) *Beyond Certainty: The Changing World of Organisations.* London: Hutchinson.

Hiltrop, J.-M. (1995) The changing psychological contract: The human resource challenge of the 1990s. *European Management Journal,* **13,** 286–294.

Jackson, P. & Van der Wielen, J. (Eds.) (in press) *New International Perspectives on Telework: From Telecommuting to the Virtual Organization.* London: Routledge.

Kessler, I. & Undy, R. (1996) *The New Employment Relationship: Examining the Psychological Contract.* London: Institute of Personnel and Development.

Kotter, J. P. (1973) The psychological contract. *California Management Review,* **15,** 91–99.

McLean Parks, J. & Kidder, D. L. (1994) "Till death us do part..." Changing work relationships in the 1990s. In: Cooper, C.L. & Rousseau, D. M. (Eds.) *Trend in Organizational Behavior,* Vol. 1. Chichester: John Wiley, pp. 111–136.

Pickard, J. (1995) Employees don't believe "psychology contract". *People Management,* **1,** 22, 5.

Robinson, S. A., Kraatz, M. S. & Rousseau, D. M. (1994) Changing obligations and the psychological contract: A longitudinal study. *Academy of Management Journal,* **37,** 137–152.

Robinson, S. L. & Rousseau, D. M. (1994) Violating the psychological contract: Not the exception but the norm. *Journal of Organizational Behavior,* **15,** 245–259.

Roe, R. A. & Schalk, R. (1996) Towards a dynamic model of the psychological contract. Tilburg: Unpublished paper work and organizational Psychology, Tilburg University.

Rousseau, D. M. (1990) New hire perspectives of their own and their employer's obligations: A study of psychological contracts. *Journal of Organizational Behavior,* **11,** 389–400.

Rousseau, D. M. (1995) *Psychological Contracts in Organizations. Understanding Written and Unwritten Agreements.* Thousand Oaks: Sage.

Rousseau, D. M. (1996a) Changing the deal while keeping the people. *Academy of Management Executive,* **10,** 50–58.

Rousseau, D. M. (1996b) Personal communication.

Rousseau, D. M. & Greller, M. M. (1994) Human resource practices: Administrative contract makers. *Human Resource Management,* **33,** 385–401.

Rousseau, D. M. & McLean Parks, J. (1993) The contracts of individuals and organizations. In: Staw, B. M. (Ed.) *Research in Organizational Behavior,* Vol. 15. Greenwich, CN: JAI Press, pp. 1–43.

Rousseau, D. M. & Wade-Benzoni, K. A. (1994) Linking strategy and human resource practices: How employees and customer contracts are created. *Human Resource Management,* **33,** 463–489.

Schalk, R., Van den Bosch, J. & Freese, C. (1994) The psychological contract of part-time and full-time employees: expectations about reciprocal obligations between the organization and the employee in the work situation. Paper presented at the 23rd International Congress of Applied Psychology, Madrid, July 1994.

Schouten, R. (1994) De individuele bepaaldheid van het psychologisch contact [Personality determinants of the psychological contract]. Tilburg: Unpublished thesis work and organizational psychology, Tilburg University.

Sims, R. R. (1994) Human resource management's role in clarifying the new psychological contract. *Human Resource Management*, **33**, 373–382.

Sugalski, T. D., Manzo, L. S. & Meadows, J. L. (1995) Resource link: Re-establishing the employment relationship in an era of downsizing. *Human Resource Management*, **34**, 389–403.

Index

Index compiled by Liz Granger

Contents of Previous Volumes